SendPoints
est. 2006

DELUXE

Foil Stamping
Embossing and Debossing
in Print Design

DELUXE

Foil Stamping Embossing and Debossing in Print Design

EDITED & PUBLISHED BY SendPoints Publishing Co., Ltd.
PUBLISHER: Lin Gengli
PUBLISHING DIRECTOR: Lin Shijian
CHIEF EDITOR: Lin Shijian
EXECUTIVE EDITOR: Huang Shaojun
EXECUTIVE ART EDITOR: Ho Waikin
PROOFREADING: James N. Powell Huang Shaojun

REGISTERED ADDRESS: Room 15A Block 9 Tsui Chuk Garden, Wong Tai Sin, Kowloon, Hong Kong
TEL: +852-35832323 / **FAX:** +852-35832448
OFFICE ADDRESS: 7F, 9th Anning Street, Jinshazhou, Baiyun District, Guangzhou, China
TEL: +86-20-89095121 / **FAX:** +86-20-89095206
BEIJING OFFICE: Room 107, Floor 1, Xiyingfang Alley, Ande Road, Dongcheng District, Beijing, China
TEL: +86-10-84139071 / **FAX:** +86-10-84139071
SHANGHAI OFFICE: Room 307, Building 1, Hong Qiang Creative Zhabei District, Shanghai, China
TEL: +86-21-63523469 / **FAX:** +86-21-63523469

SALES MANAGER: Sissi
TEL: +86-20-81007895
EMAIL: overseas01@sendpoints.cn
WEBSITE: www.sendpoints.cn / www.spbooks.cn

ISBN 978-988-77572-3-8

Printed and bound in China.

Contents

FOIL STAMPING

Foil stamping (also known as foil application, flat stamping, hot stamping, gold stamping, blocking, and leafing) is a popular printing technology. It uses heat and pressure to apply metallic foil to materials such as paper, wood, and leather. This printing technique helps to increase the printed media's added value, boost their recognition, and endow them with an air of authenticity. This section discusses mainly the application of hot foil stamping (a type of foil stamping) on paper.

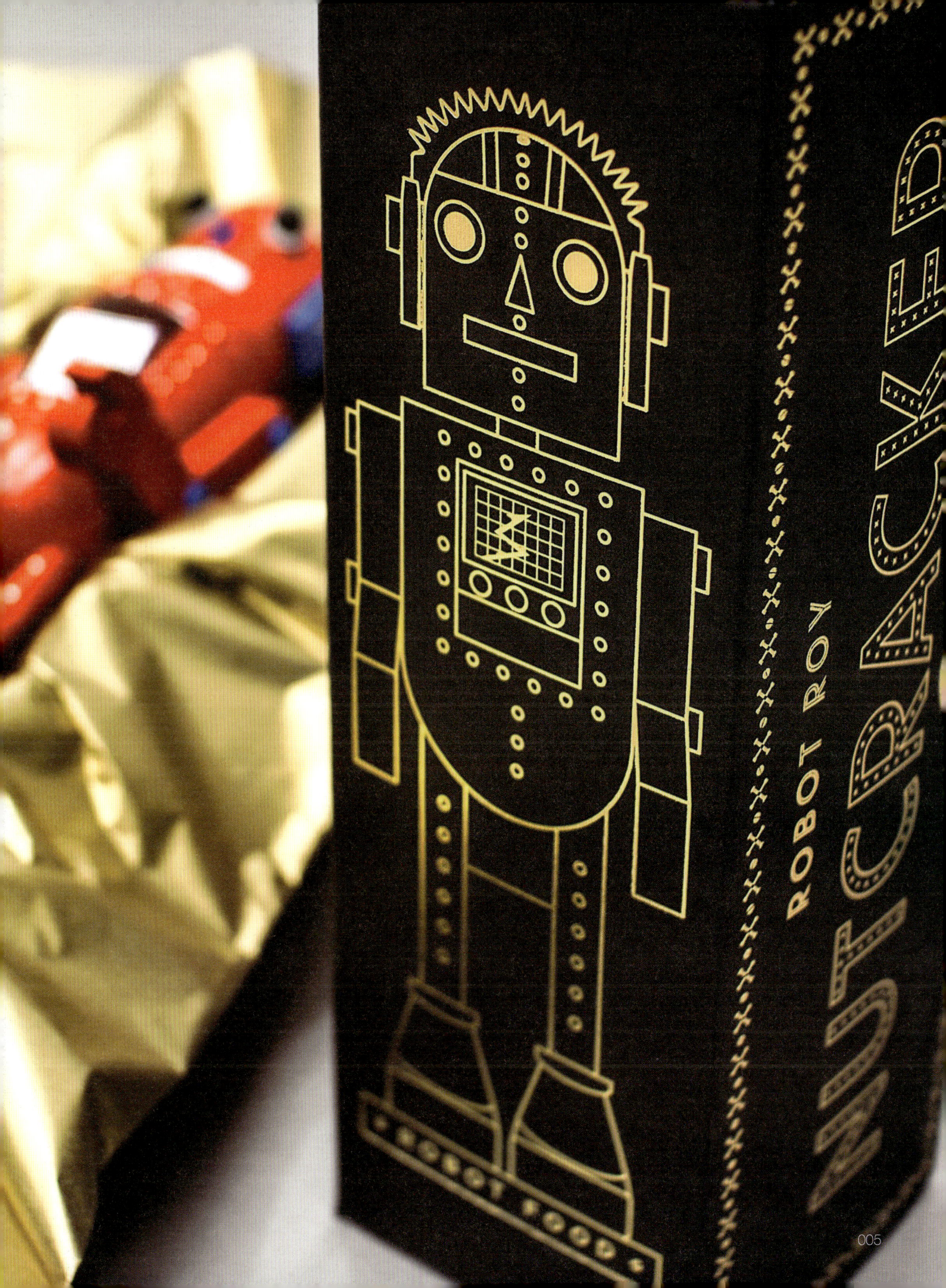
ROBOT ROY
ROBOT FOOD

How It Works

To facilitate a better understanding of the technique's process, we have described it simply. The foil is positioned between the heated metal die and the paper receiving the foil. The die presses the foil onto the paper, and the heat activates the adhesive. Under pressure, the foil fuses onto the surface of the paper and is released from the mylar carrier everywhere the raised images or texts have pressed. When the pressure stops, the adhesive cools and solidifies quickly, and the foil permanently adheres to the substrate (as shown below).

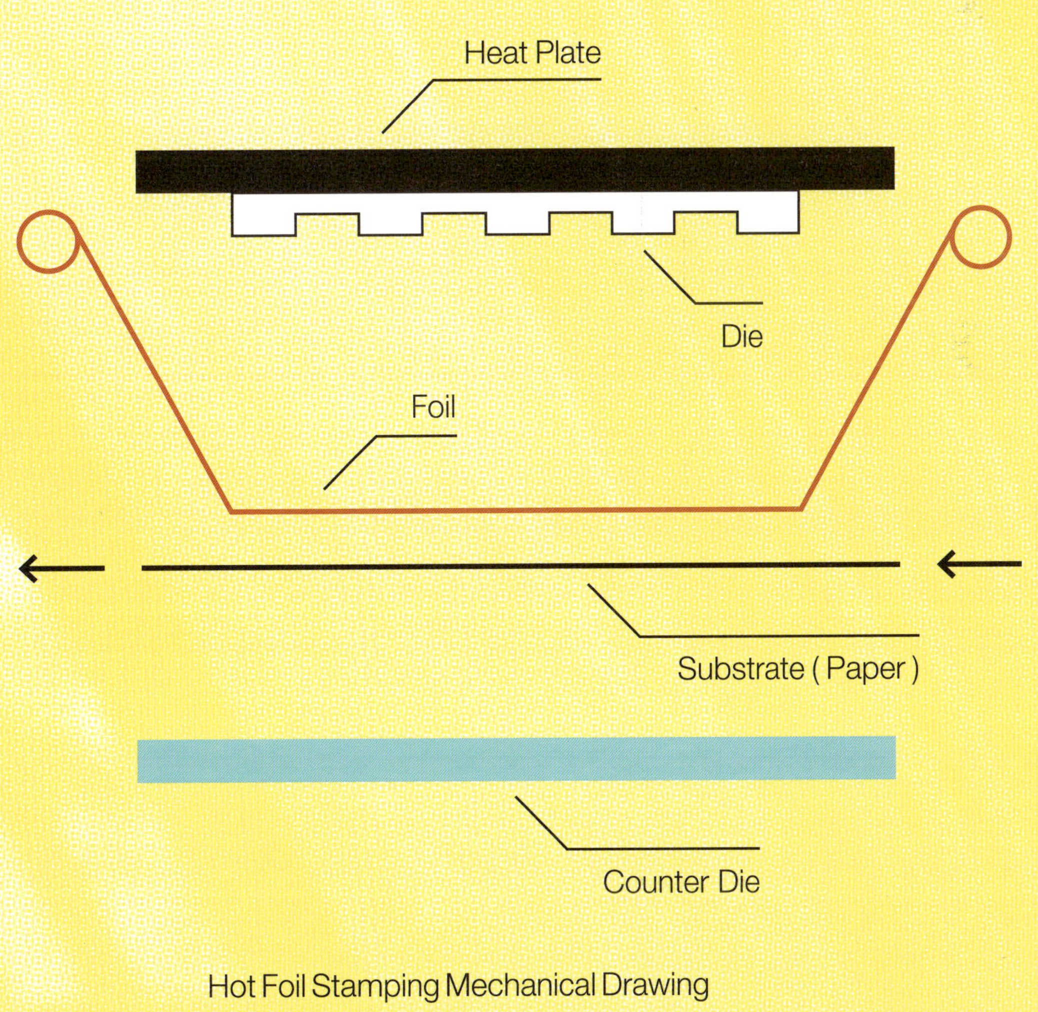

Hot Foil Stamping Mechanical Drawing

What You Need

For a hot-foil-stamping process, you need to prepare foil, die, and a hot-foil-stamping machine.

Foil

Foils are polymer films coated with a thin layer of metal, which is performed using a vacuum-metallizing process. There are two main foils, one is a general foil and the other is laser foil.

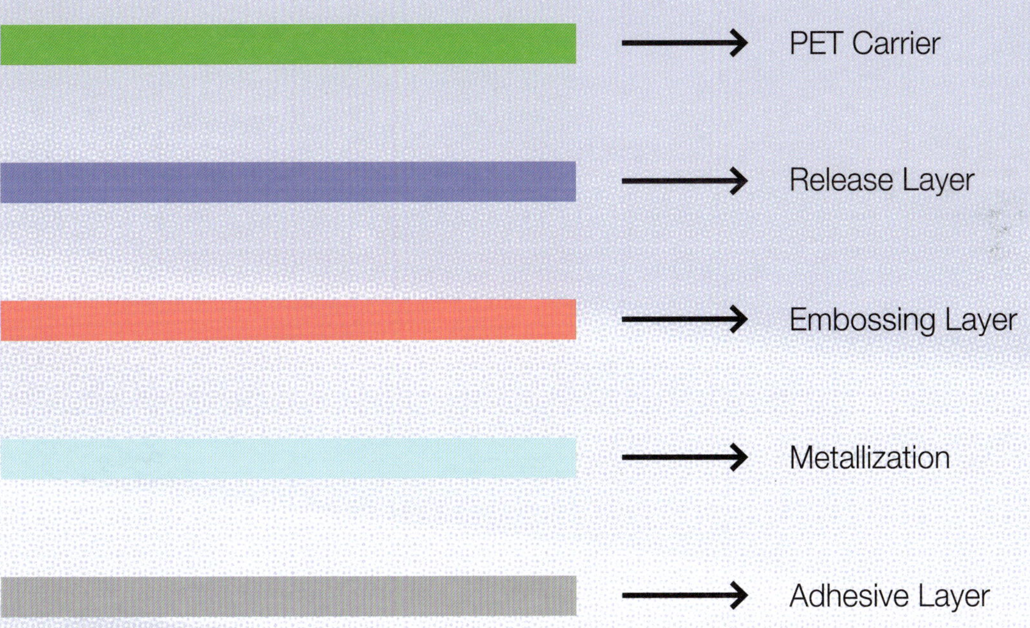

Structure of Foil

Zinc Die

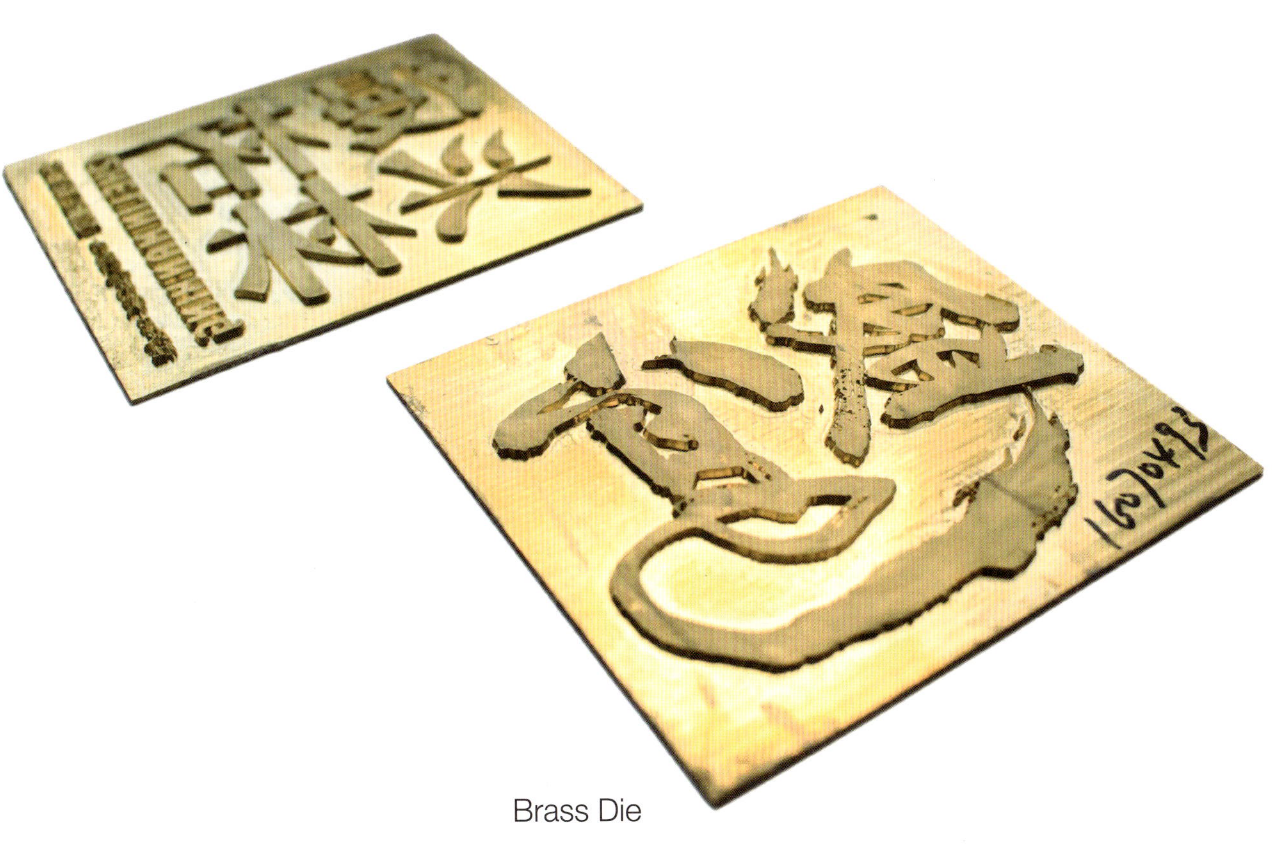

Brass Die

Die

A foil-stamping die is a plate etched with printed images. The dies are available in a variety of materials. Here we present four of them: zinc, magnesium, copper, and brass.

Zinc and magnesium are relatively soft and low cost, but not durable. Dies made of them are the best choice for short runs.

Copper wears better than zinc and magnesium, but is not etched as deeply. Coppers dies are good for foil stamping with fine details.

Brass is durable than copper and best for medium to long imprint runs. They are excellent for foil stamping with fine details.

Hot–Foil–Stamping Machine

There are two kinds of stamping machines: manual foil-stamping machine and automatic foil-stamping machine.

Manual Foil-Stamping Machine

The manual one is economical and comes in a small size. It is also easily to operate. It is, however, not qualified for high-quality foil stamping. In this aspect, the automatic one surpasses its manual counterpart. They generate not only fine foil-stamping effects, but also have excellent control over heat, pressure, and time when stamping.

Automatic Foil-Stamping Machine

How To Attain Control Quality

Heat

Generally, the heat for flat foil-stamping ranges from 70°C to 110°C and 140°C to 150°C for round foil stamping. If the heat is too low, the foil will not fuse and stick. If the heat is too high, the foil may bubble or blister and change color, or the images may blur, or the paper may distort.

Time

Time adds another factor vital to the final stamping result. The optimal situation is to produce the most satisfactory stamping result in the least time. Generally, the stamping speed for a manual foil-stamping machine is 600 - 700 sheets/hr, with 3,500 - 5,000 sheets/hr for an automatic one.

Pressure

The pressure depends on the thickness and size of the substrate and the type of foil stamping. A proper pressure would satisfy these aspects: clean imprint, good gloss in foil, no flaking in decoration, and no filling in. If there are more than two parts of images with dramatically different sizes on one single die, the unit pressure and the ability of the substrate to stand the pressure should be carefully considered. The larger the stamping area, the greater the pressure that should be used.

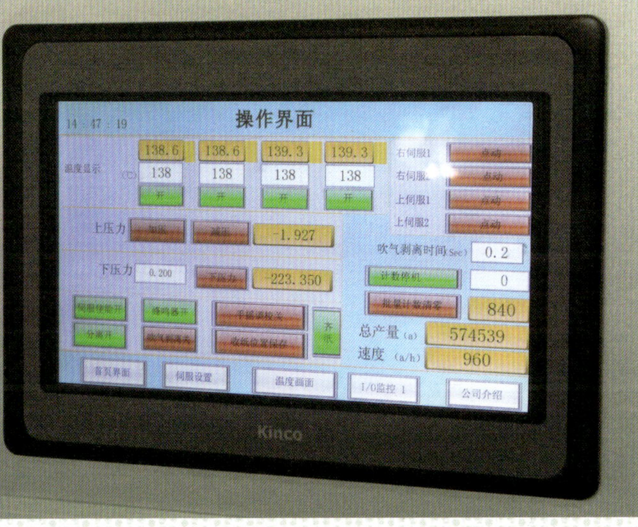

Steps of Foil Stamping

- Preparation Work Before Stamping
- Die Setting
- Adjusting Speed, Temperature, and Heat
- Printing a Sample
- Sample Approving
- Formal Print Start

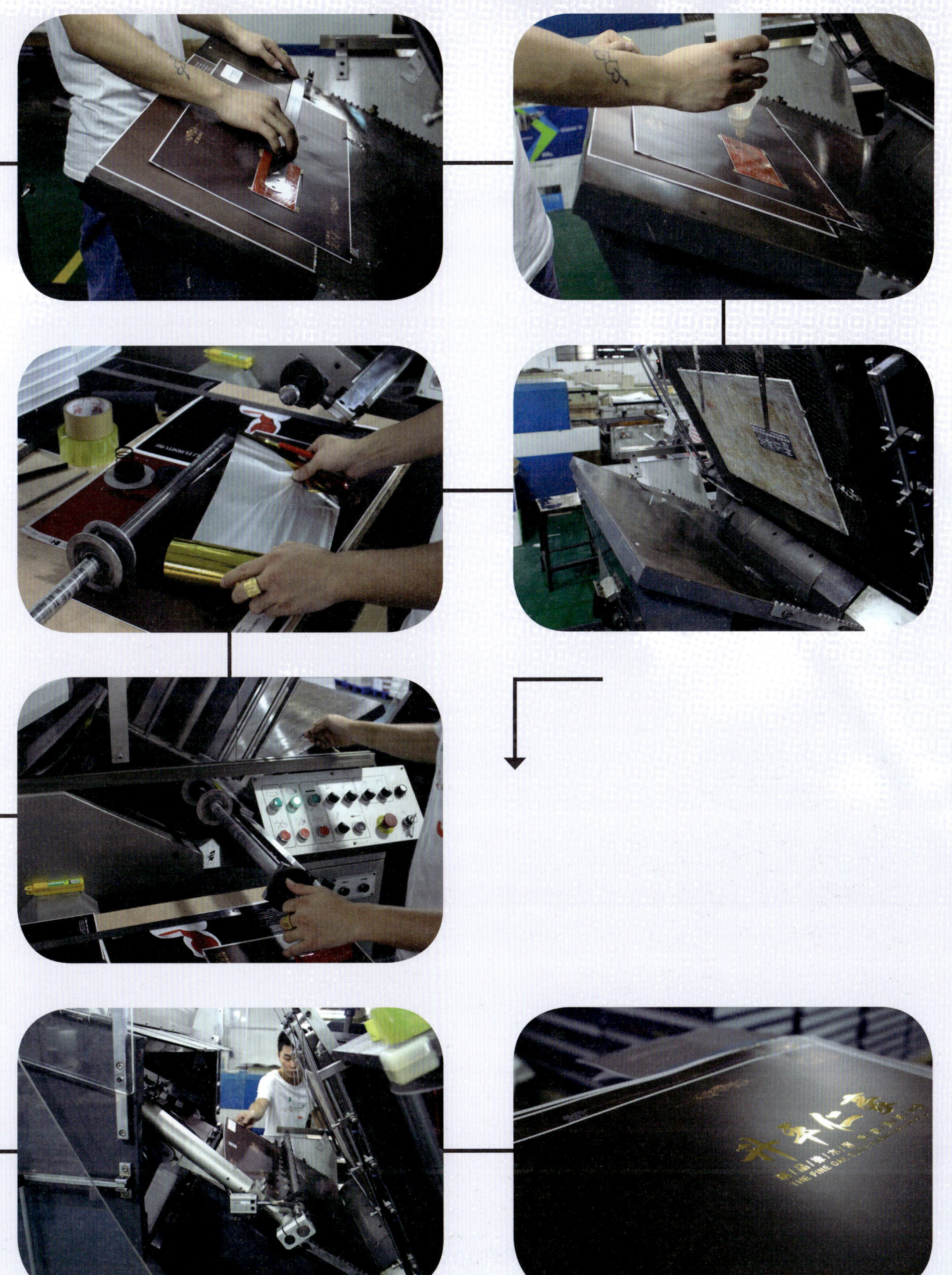

Types of Foil Stamping

Apart from hot foil printing, discussed above, more types of foil stamping have evolved with the development of printing technology. Here we briefly introduce three more types: cold foil printing, foil embossing, and hologram foil.

Cold Foil Printing

Cold foil is a process that uses only pressure to transfer foil to the paper or other substrates. The first step is to apply an ultraviolet cold foil adhesive to the substrate. An ultraviolet dryer then cures the adhesive, which becomes tacky. The second step is to press together the foil carrier and the substrate covered by the printed adhesive. Thus the foil will stick to the adhesive on the substrate and an image with a bright foil is created. The last step is to varnish or encapsulate the surface of cold foil images, which generates a protective layer and makes for a durable surface.

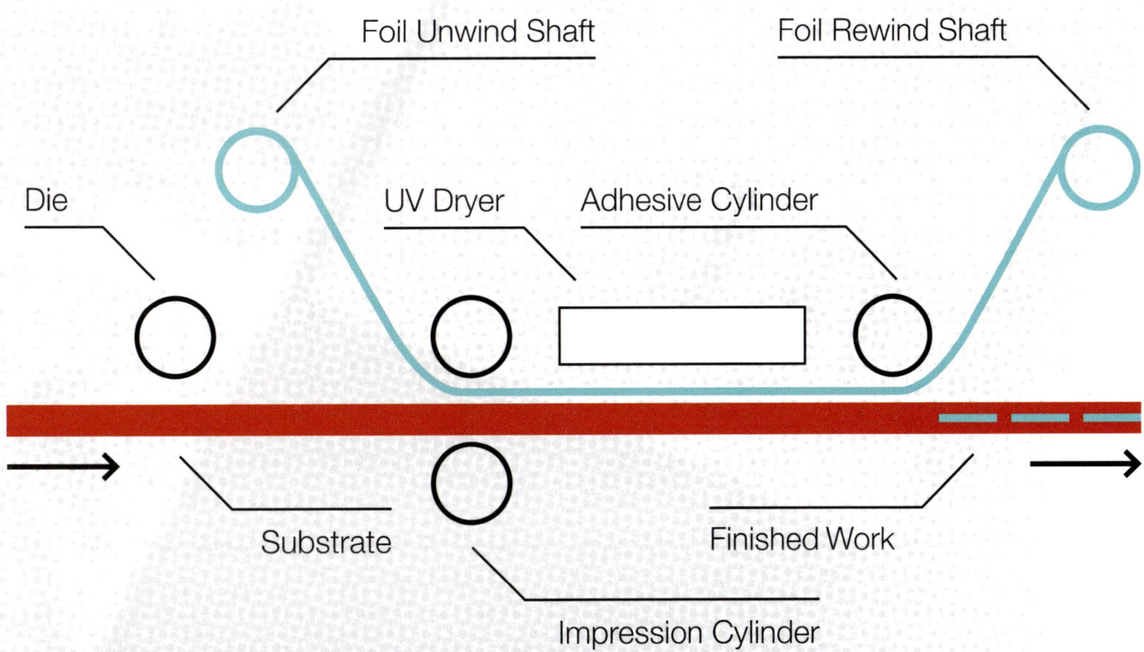

Cold Foil Printing Mechanical Drawing

Foil Embossing

Foil embossing unites foil stamping and embossing into one press pass, through the use of a combination die, usually a brass-sculptured embossing die with a foil breakage edge to end the image area. This technique finishes the foil printing and embossing at one time, reducing the registration problem and improving productivity.

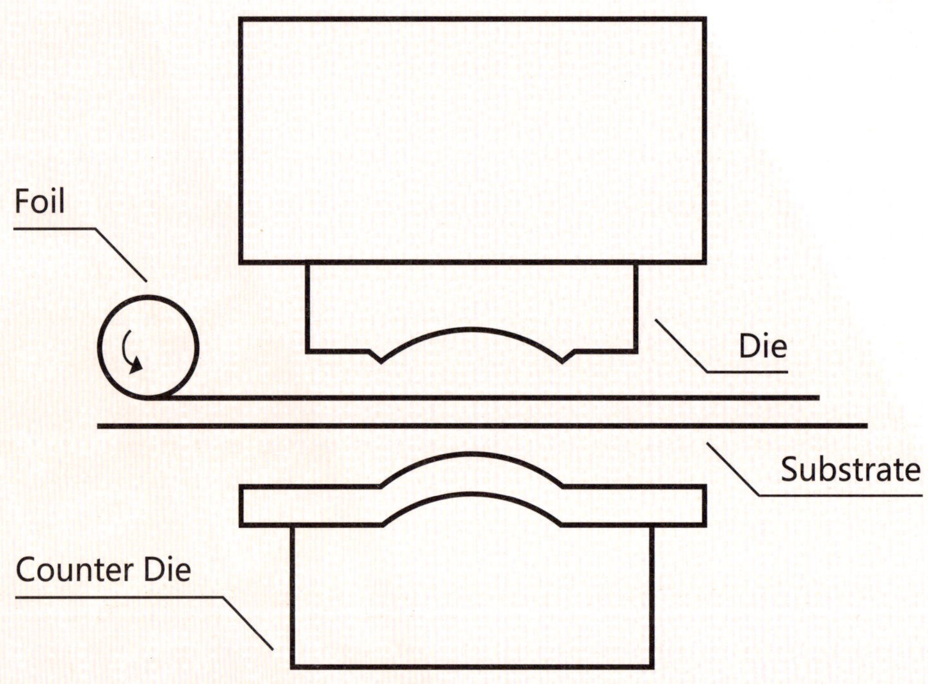

Foil Embossing Mechanical Drawing

HAPPY
Best wishes for the year to come!
福祿壽囍
LONGEVITY & HEALTH
SINCERELY
ERS
MONKEY
2016

Hologram Foil

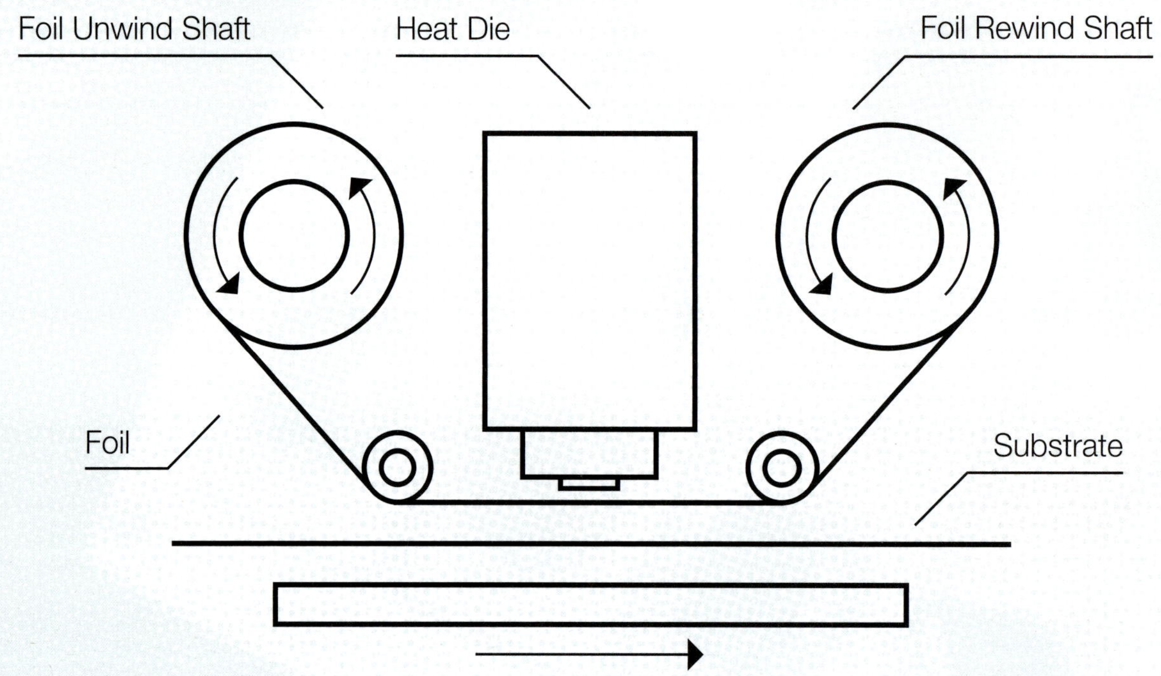

Hologram Foil Mechanical Drawing

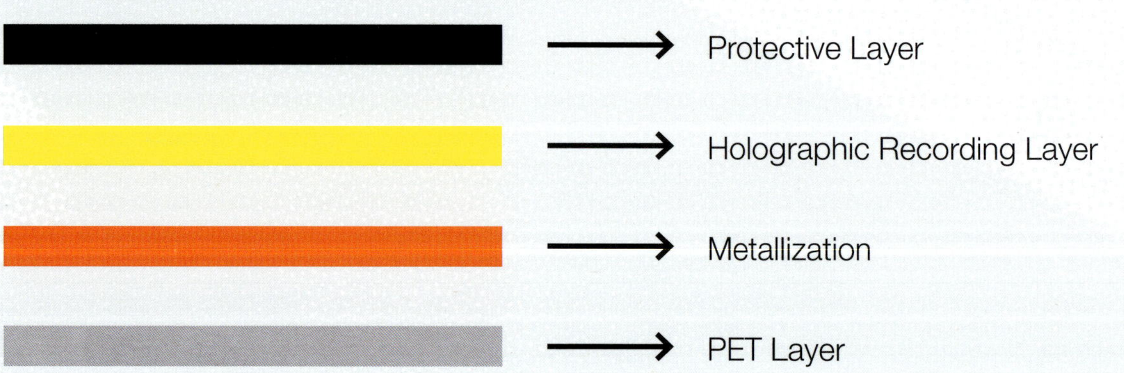

Structure of Holographic Foil

Hologram foil is a printing technique to apply holographic foil on a printed substrate. When the printed die is heated, the heat-sensitive adhesive layer and the release layer of the holographic foil placed between the die and the substrate will fuse. Under pressure, the information layer with holographic gratings releases from the polyester layer and sticks to the substrate.

Holographic foil comes in two forms: non-registered holographic foil and registered holographic foil. The main reason for their application to the printed matter is to deter the counterfeiting of documents and to increase perceived value.

Good Design

Design MURMURE

MURMURE design studio embraces the philosophy that "behind every good project lies a good client." When it comes to their new business cards, their philosophy is conveyed and highlighted via graphic and printing qualities. Other information and the capitalized *M*, combined with various sizes of dots on the reverse side, are printed by debossing to make for premium cards displaying impressive depth. While the foil-stamped dots on the cards add a sense of liveliness.

good design
– is for good
clients

good design
– is for good
clients.

good design
– is for good
clients
Paul Ressencourt
& Julien Alirol
Directeurs Artistiques
09.80.56.81.30
contact@murmure.me
www.murmure.me

Paul Ressencourt
& Julien Alirol
Directeurs Artistiques
09.80.56.81.30
contact@murmure.me
www.murmure.me
— is for
clients

The Golden Camera 2015

Design Paperlux GmbH

This stationery set was designed for the Golden Camera 2015, an event dated back to 1966.
The event name Golden Camera was embossing-printed on golden and ultra-black paper, using a modern typeface Grotesk Walsheim. What accompanies the name is the lettering Fünfzig ("fifty" in German), that was created solely for this event to underline its history. It is discreetly used, always in a foil-stamping form. The strong colors black and gold enhanced by high print quality bring about a formal and high-profile event.

DIE GOLDENE KAMERA VON HÖRZU
Fünfzig
50 JAHRE
Die 50. Verleihung der GOLDENEN KAMERA von HÖRZU am Freitag, den 27. Februar 2015
A
D
Die Dinnerparty anlässlich der 50. Verleihung der GOLDENEN KAMERA von HÖRZU am Freitag, den 27. Februar 2015
22:30 UHR
Dinnerparty
Hamburg Messe, Messeplatz 1, Halle A1
KAMERA VON HÖRZU
HÖRZU
F
17:30 UHR
Champagner-Empfang im Foyer der Hamburg Messe, Messeplatz 1, Halle A1
19:30 UHR
Preisverleihung
ANSCHLIESSEND
Dinnerparty

Guinness Identity

Design Design Bridge

Guinness, a world-renowned brewery updated its identity to emphasize its heritage of craftsmanship. Each element of the new identity has its own story to tell, such as the "estd. 1759" type, which can be traced back to the metal-stamped lettering imprinted in the ironwork and oak barrels at the Guinness Storehouse. The new harp icon is beautifully executed, with the woodcut-esque, one-color style making for a strikingly elegant design. Touch-friendly letterpress highlights the craftsmanship, combining metallic inks, debossing, and foil blocking. All of these help provide an alluring presentation.

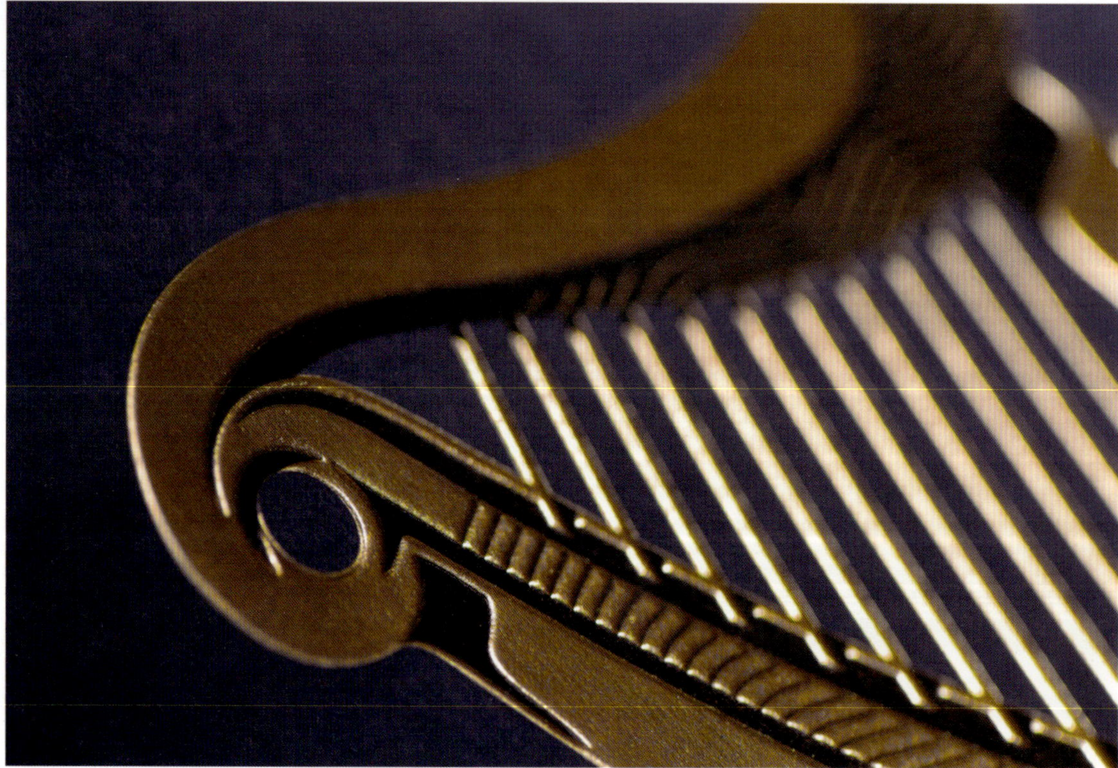

ESTD 1759

GUINNESS™

ST JAMES'S GATE DUBLIN, IRELAND

Arth Guinness™

A Royal Letterhead - Stationary Design

Design ONOGRIT Design Studio

For Ghanaian king Nana Kwadwo Owusu, ONOGRIT designed a stationary set for his official correspondence. It consists of a letterhead, business cards, and invitations. The visuals display traditional royal Ghanaian symbols that are developed into a consistent set of icons. These icons are all foil printed throughout the design to enhance premium quality. The design team also created various achromatic patterns, printing them out as posters.

COQUETTE
CACAO
FAIR TRADE
MILK CHOCOLATE
100% PREMIUM GHANA CACAO
YOU ARE INVITED
TO CELEBRATE WITH THE KING

Chinese New Year Card 2016

Design Lee Chieh-Ting

Lee Chieh-Ting designed this series of warm cards for the 2016 Chinese New Year.
In the design, such elements as a New Year' scroll, firecracker, and lantern are used as iconic symbols. Because 2016 is the Year of the Monkey in Chinese culture, the Chinese character 猴 (meaning "monkey"), as well as illustrated monkeys appear on the cards. The cards have variously colored backgrounds, for the designer wants to deliver his best wishes to his friends around Asia having different color preferences. The body is printed with gold-foil stamping. Thus, the color gold highlights and enhances this elegant design.

Best wishes for the year to come!
福祿壽囍
LONGEVITY & HEALTH
HAPPY
NEW YEAR
CHEERS
SINCERELY
HAPPY MONKEY YEAR
猴
2016
...'s words belong to last year's language
...ear's words await another voice.
...end is to make a beginning.
— T.S. Eliot

CHEERS
Best wishes for the year to come!
LONGEVITY & HEALTH
HAPPY
SINCERELY
MONKEY YEAR
猴
2016
NEW YEAR
ong to last year's language
s await another voice.
to make a beginning.
— T.S. Eliot

Fortnum & Mason

Design Design Bridge

Fortnum & Mason sells a line of handmade English chocolates. Their new packaging is designed to pay homage to the exquisite contents awaiting within. To echo the Georgian grandeur of Fortnum & Mason's iconic store, Design Bridge created a series of patterns featuring a menagerie of English flora and fauna and presented them on paper influenced by Georgian Styling. The gold-foil finish greatly contributes to the gorgeous design, lending a multi-sensory and multi-layered presentation that tempts you to look — and then look again.

FORTNUM & MASON
PICCADILLY SINCE 1707
Chocolate-Covered Stem Ginger
these handcrafted Milk and Dark Chocolate Stem Gingers are feisty, spicy and
in copper pans, our recipe uses the finest ingredients for a texture and taste that
rich and velvety taste of chocolate as it perfectly captures the depth of soft yet
Take a daring bite into your spicy side.

FORTNUM & MASON
NUT
SELECTION
A Scrumptious Selection of Nuts Covered
in Milk and Dark Chocolate

ROSE & VIOLET

FORTNUM & MASON
CHOCOLATE-COVERED
STEM GINGER

FORTNUM & MASON
ASSORTED
CREAMS

Wang & Cheng's Wedding Invitation

Design Ting Bin Wang

In Chinese culture, wedding invitation design tends to adhere to fixed conventions, preferring two colors: bright red and gold. Wang breaks away from such constrictions, choosing instead a peachy-pink color card with silver-foil stamping, symbolizing sweetness. Wang then reinterprets the Chinese traditional wedding pattern of *龍鳳吉祥* (Auspicious Dragon and Phoenix), modernizing it so that the complex traditional image is translated into simplified lines. Echoing this elegant rebirth of these images, Wang uses decorative lines for the typeface, inserting a new element into the conventional format.

WEDDING
BANQUET
5.25
SUNDAY
PM 12:00
WE ARE GETTING
MARRIED
YOU ARE INVITED
TINGSIN

Flashtones

Design Lilkudley

Flashtones is a fresh brand based in the Czech Republic and producing colorful socks sold as single pieces. Their playful packaging box looks like a normal paper towel box, but what you pull out from it is not tissues but socks. The faces of the box display the logo of the sock brand while the golden foil detail highlights the brand in a cardboard background.

FLASHTONES
FLASHTONES
FLASHTONES
FLASHTONES
FLASHTONES
FLASHTONES

FLASHTONES

Miin Brewery

Design ContentFormContext

Miin Brewery is a traditional Korean traditional rice wine brewery at Paju. Following a direct approach, its expressive logo depicts, with elegant lines, a traditional wine container and a brewery. For Miin, inspired by old maps from the Joseon Dynasty, the design team drew a Miin Brewery Map for the graphic, using four Chinese characters: 美, 人, 酒, and 家. Miin means *beautiful woman* in Korean. Thus, they endowed the characters with delicately curved lines to deliver images of beauty further enhanced by foil embossing.

MIIN BREWERY
MIIN BREWERY
TRD MRK
Alc.10% 500ml

DIZ-DIZ Microwave Popcorn

Design Tatabi Studio

DIZ-DIZ is a brand of gourmet popcorn offering four unique and delicious flavors. DIZ-DIZ's branding incorporates the soft colors of the four flavors, creating a colorful and delicate result. To enhance the brand's luxurious and gourmet emphasis, the designers combined white-marble colors with metallic materials. This yields a luxurious and elegant feel.

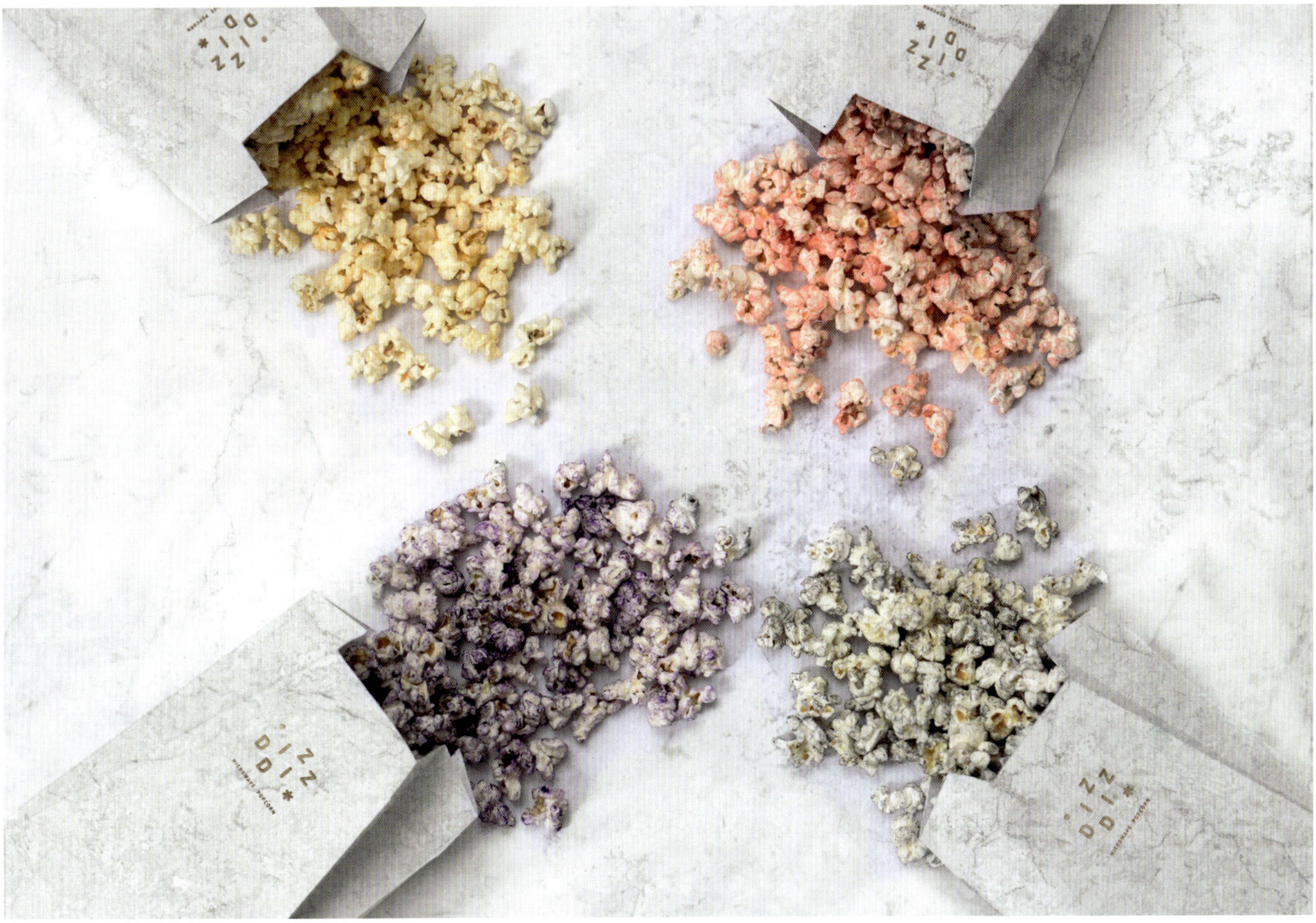

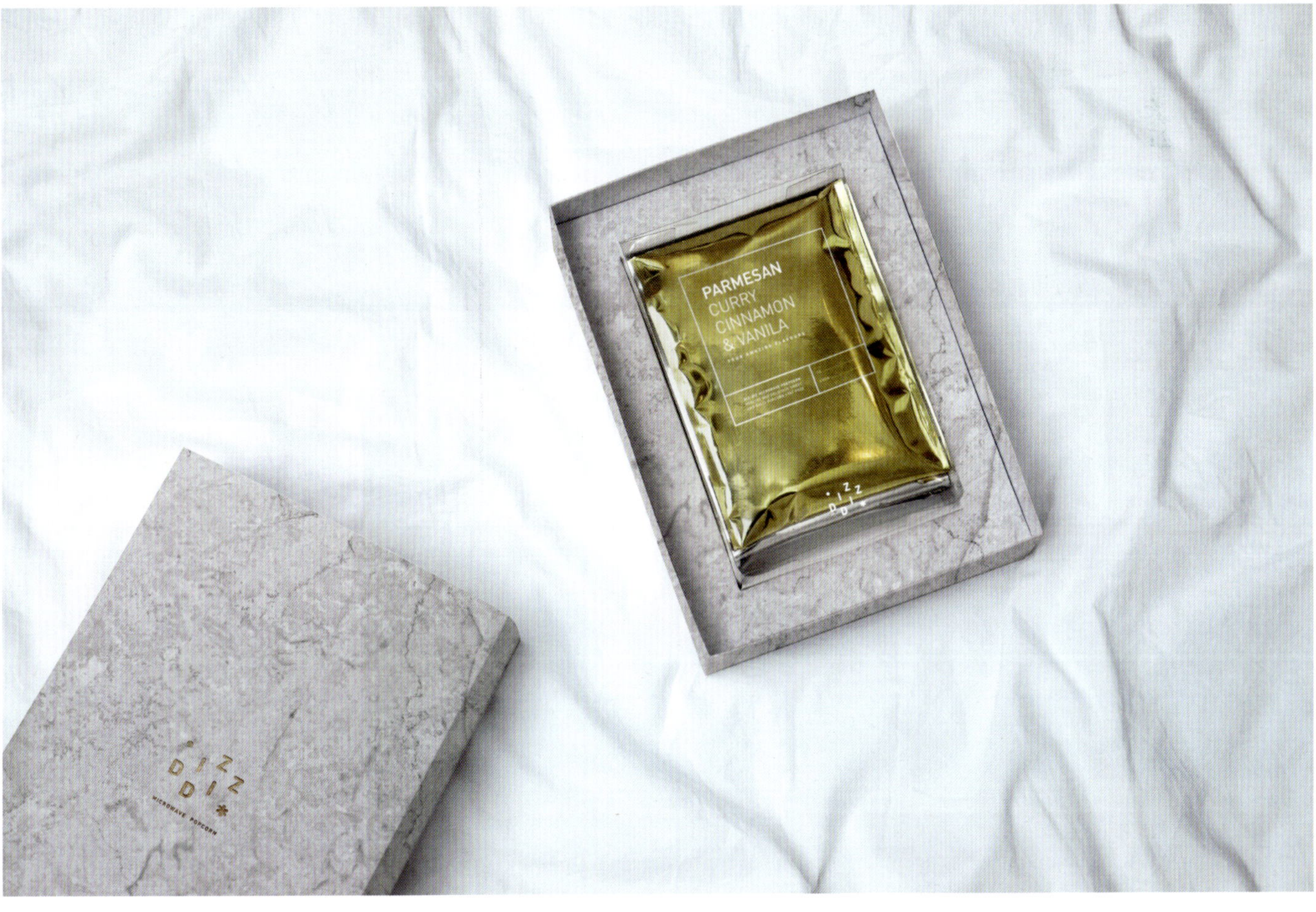
PARMESAN
CURRY
CINNAMON
& VANILA

Kamonishiki

Design Suisei

Kamonishiki is a Japanese liquor company. One of its lines, ***金箔入祝酒***, is produced for celebrations. Considering the celebratory setting, the line's labels incorporate the icon of a pine, in Japanese culture a symbol of longevity. The pine pattern appears in letterpress and functions as a background on which the liquor's name is printed in gold.

加茂錦
Festive Sake
infused with gold
金箔入

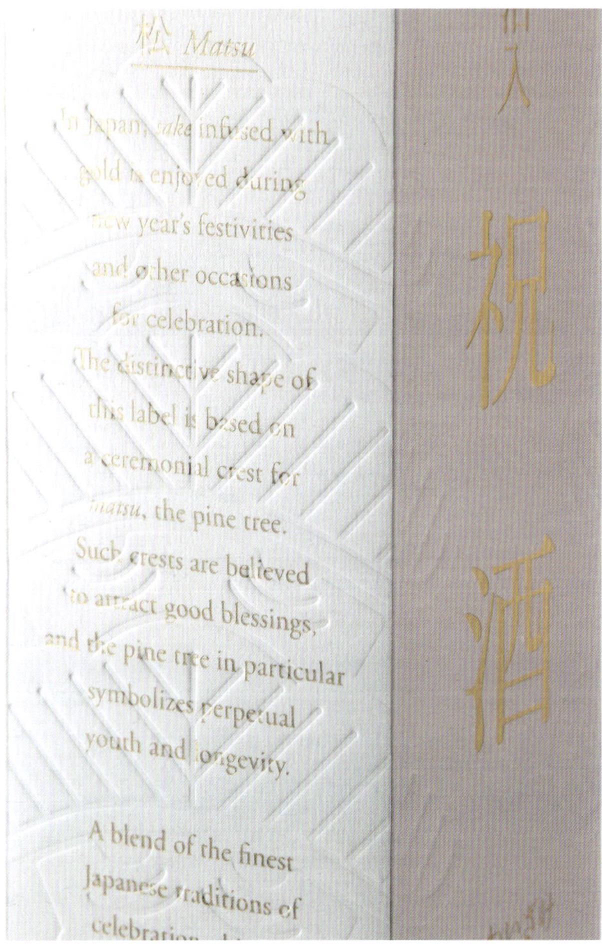
松 Matsu
new year's festivities
for celebration.
matsu, the pine tree.
A blend of the finest
祝酒

Vinos Fríos del Año

Design DEO

Vinos Fríos del Año are fresh, young wines from Chile's Curicó Valley. DEO designed a label with the vintage year as the main graphic element. The vintage is highlighted by a hot-foil finish and framed by the brand name, J.A. Jofré.

J. A.
JOFRÉ
Vinos Fríos del Año
TINTO
MALBEC
CARIÑENA
CARMENERE
TEMPRANILLO
2015
Vino de Chile
BLANCO
SEMILLÓN
SAUVIGNON VERT
ROSADO
GARNACHA
PETIT VERDOT
J O F R É

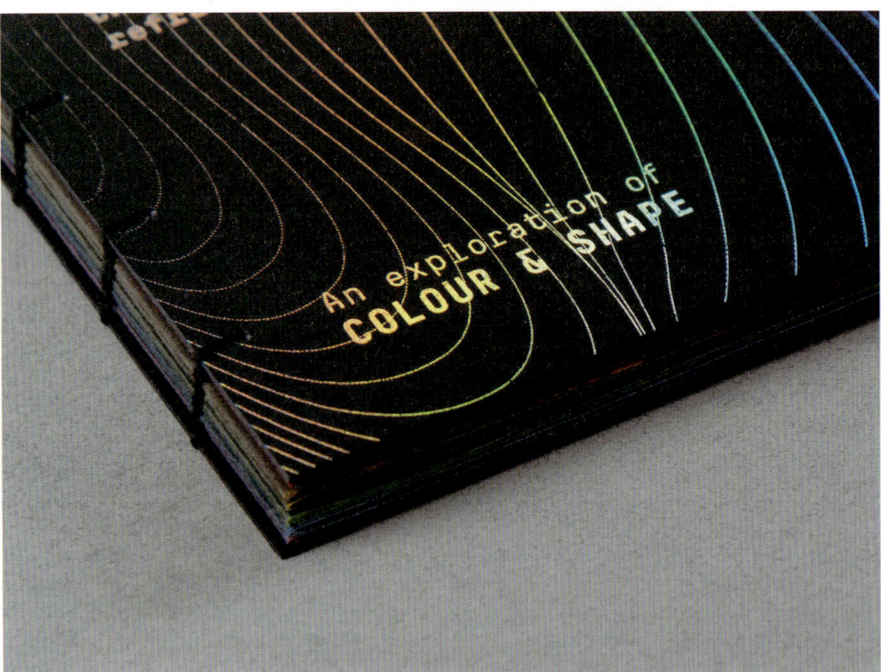

Harlow Light Trail

Design Ryan Panchal

Panchal created this dazzling work for D&AD: Reimagine Your Hometown. Inspired by his hometown Harlow, the birthplace of fiber optics (which transmits information via light), Panchal centered his work around light and expressed the idea via a colorful palette based on the diffraction of white light into the six pure colors. For the printed materials, Panchal used holographic foil that changes color depending on how light strikes its surface. The holographic foil finish perfectly reflects the light-centered design concept.

HARLOW
Light
Trail
CONNECT WITH HARLOW
Download the app to create
a colourful light sculpture
in the centre of Harlow.
Available on the
App Store
HARLOW
Light
Trail
CONNECT WITH HARLOW
Download the app to create
a colourful light sculpture
in the centre of Harlow.
Available on the
App Store
CONNECT WITH HARLOW
Download the app to create
a colourful light sculpture
in the centre of Harlow.

YUHENG TEA

Design Onion Design Associates

YUHENG Tea is a small-scale, family-owned tea producer in Taiwan. The logo is based on the Chinese character *恆*, taken from their brand name, *有恆焙茶*. It is also a graphical representation of tea leaves inside a cup as well as tea leaves lying on a bamboo tray during the withering process. Highlighted in a raised form, the logo states the tea's quality.

阿里山金萱
ALISHAN JIN XUAN

Borandes

Design DEO

Borandes is a project blending two winemaking styles, one French, the other Chilean. Therefore, the label features iconic elements from each country in order to represent that duality combined in one bottle. The key element reflecting this intermingling is printed foil — the label's focal point.

2013
Chile
Bor—
andes
ASSEMBLAGE
Cabernet Sauvignon
Cabernet Franc
Carmenere

Roasting Masters

Located in Seoul, Roasting Masters is a coffee roasting company with a new identity for their new business, Bean to Bar Chocolate. Considering that all beans for the company hail from Latin America, the packaging design employs vivid color palettes and patterns inspired by Latin culture. On each packaging box, a solid logo is accentuated in a metallic tone. Then, as a final touch, one coffee bean is added to the logo as a reference to the company's nature.

Foil Stamping

From a cacao tree to a chocolate bar

— *by Roasting Masters* —

Material Art Fair

Design Anagrama

Material Art Fair is a contemporary venue dedicated to emerging practices in Mexico City. The fair's branding features a bright color palette and combination of patterns and processes. Hologram foil detail augments the color scheme, making lending a luminous dynamic.

MATERIAL
CITY
MEXICO
R—SVP
8

MATERIAL ART FAIR
MATERIAL
CITY
MEXICO

Valentto

Design Anagrama

Valentto is Olivarera Italo-Mexicana's virgin olive oil brand, destined for industrial kitchen and restaurant use. To counteract Valentto's original industrial look, Anagrama added beautiful Italian landscapes as background. The Italian country scenery not only serves to balance the industrial coldness this brand might otherwise suggest, by exuding natural warmth, an air of family, and tradition. The logotype fits snuggly within a diamond, lending it a compact and symmetrical look. Hot-pressed gold foil and uncoated unbleached paper speak for the brand's high quality of cold-pressed, all-natural extra virgin olive oil.

VALENTTO
ACEITE DE OLIVA
FERNANDO BORTETTI
+52 (686) 555 1120 / 02
FERNANDO@VALENTTO.COM
VALENTTO.COM
AVENUE COSTA RICA N°60
COLONIA CUAUHTEMOC NTE
CP 21200
MEXICALI, BAJA CALIFORNIA

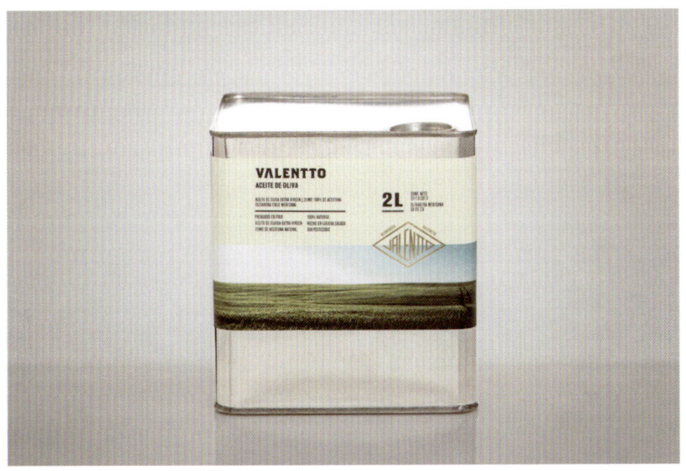
VALENTTO
ACEITE DE OLIVA
2L

El Montero

Design Anagrama

El Montero is a restaurant located in Saltillo Coahuila, a city close to Mexico's northern border. Its menu is inspired by regional food and features a solid-black leather cover on which the logo is golden hot stamped. This golden element also adorns other parts such as the letter head. What further unifies the stationery set is the raised brand name in circle typography. The black-gold color palette and the chess-like pattern create a modern style for the identity.

MONTERO NUEVA COCINA RÚSTICA
HIDALGO SUR No.211 ZONA CENTRO
SALTILLO COAHUILA CP 25000— MX
T 844 410 3535
ELMONTERO.MX
INFO@ELMONTERO.MX
NUEVA MONTERO
COCINA RÜSTICA

Chong Kio Ginseng

Design 2tigers

Chong Kio ginseng is a product line produced by Macau-based company Chong Kio Co.
With a view to modernizing the old brand, the new identity of Chong Kio ginseng is designed around the initials of Chong Kio and developed it into blossoming patterns. The golden detail of the pattern and packaging illumines the design.

中僑參茸
CHONG KIO
FARMACIA CHINESA CO.
EST. 1950

中僑參茸
CHONG KIO
FARMACIA CHINESA CO.
est. 1950

Chocolate Concierge

Design Anagraphic

Chocolate Concierge cares about their beans origins, fair trade, and each process that leads up to placing their chocolates in your hands. Their packaging illustrates this philosophy in the drawing of a coffee tree, on which the beans are highlighted in foil. The golden trees within the box echo to the outside foil, while adding a chic touch to the design.

chocolate
CONCIERGE
PROUDLY SERVING YOU WITH FRESH, ARTISAN CHOCOLATES
chocolate
CONCIERGE

chocolate
CONCIERGE

Illustrations of Good Taste

Design Maria Ponomareva

This packaging design communicates the subtle variations of honey via black-and-white pencil illustrations. Color is held in abeyance in this case to mirror the naturalness and purity of the organic contents. The logo, however, reigns above the illustrations, printed in shinning golden foil, sweetening the presentation with a rainbow of colors.

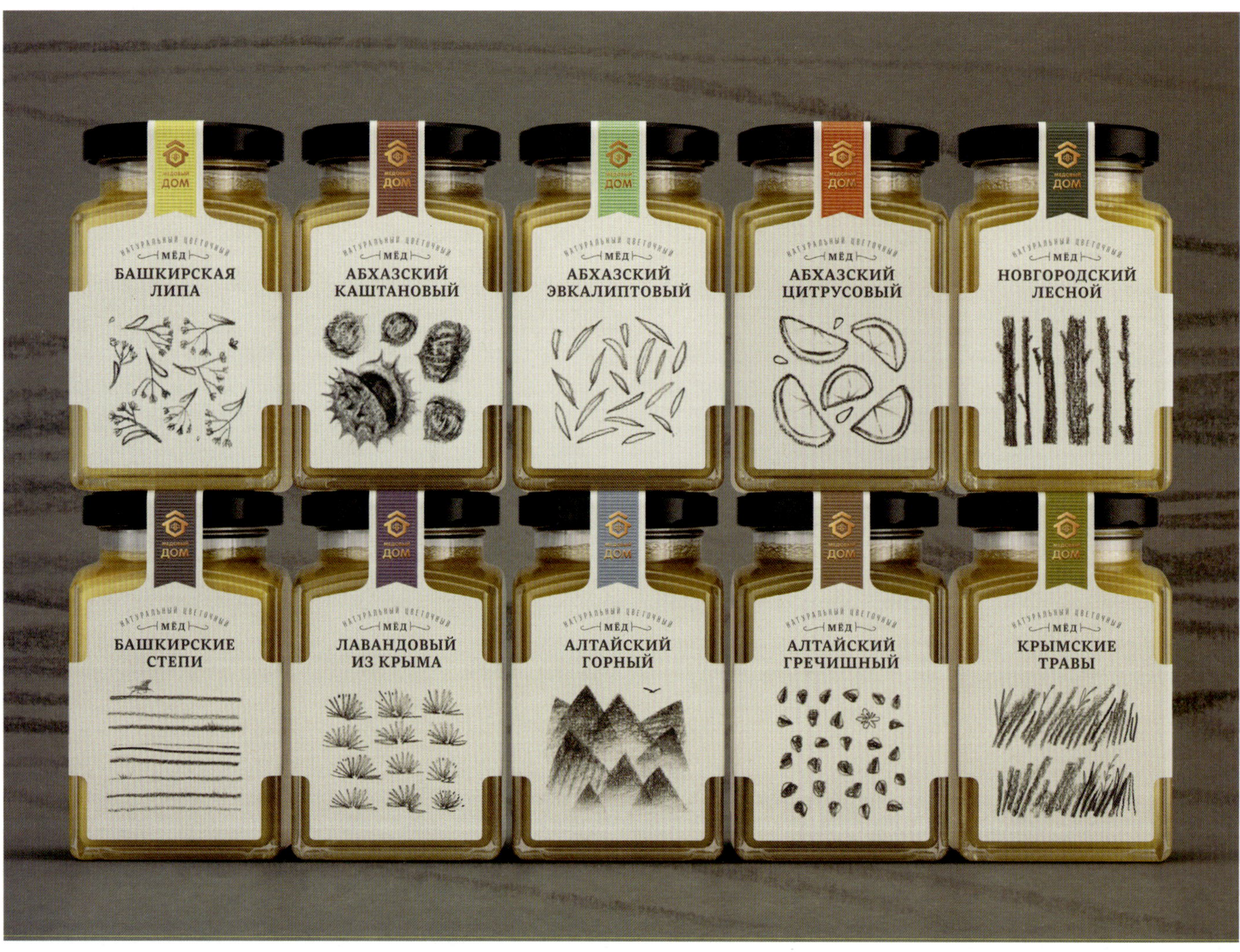

No Wine No See

Design Nio Ni

This wine packaging offers a breath of fresh air among labels all about heritage and terroir. A fun, illustrative set of labels developed by Nio Ni, it expresses a rich variety of feelings and emotions. At the center of the vivid illustrations shines the glittering gold of brand name, illuminating the unique design.

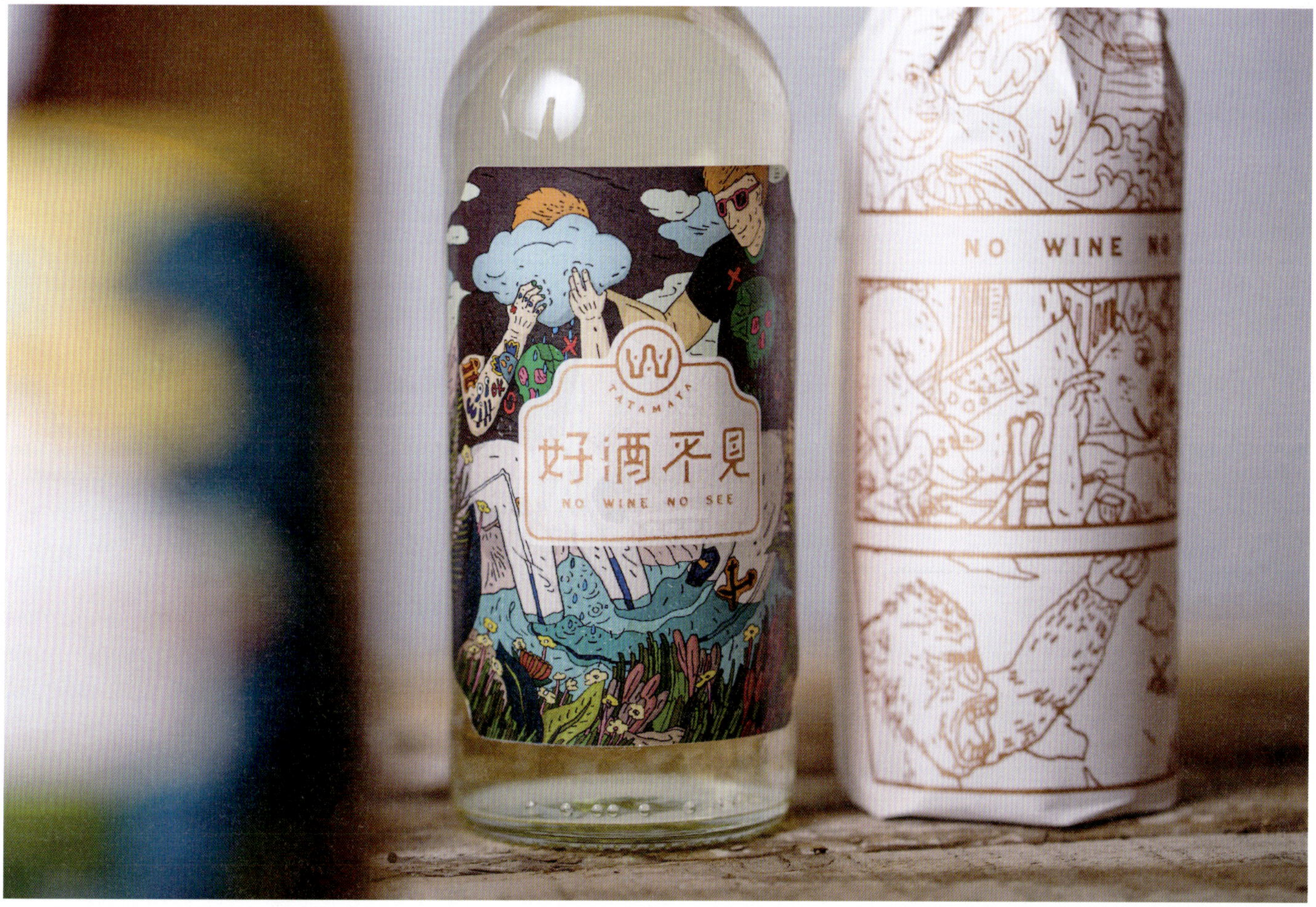
好酒不見
NO WINE NO SEE
NO WINE NO

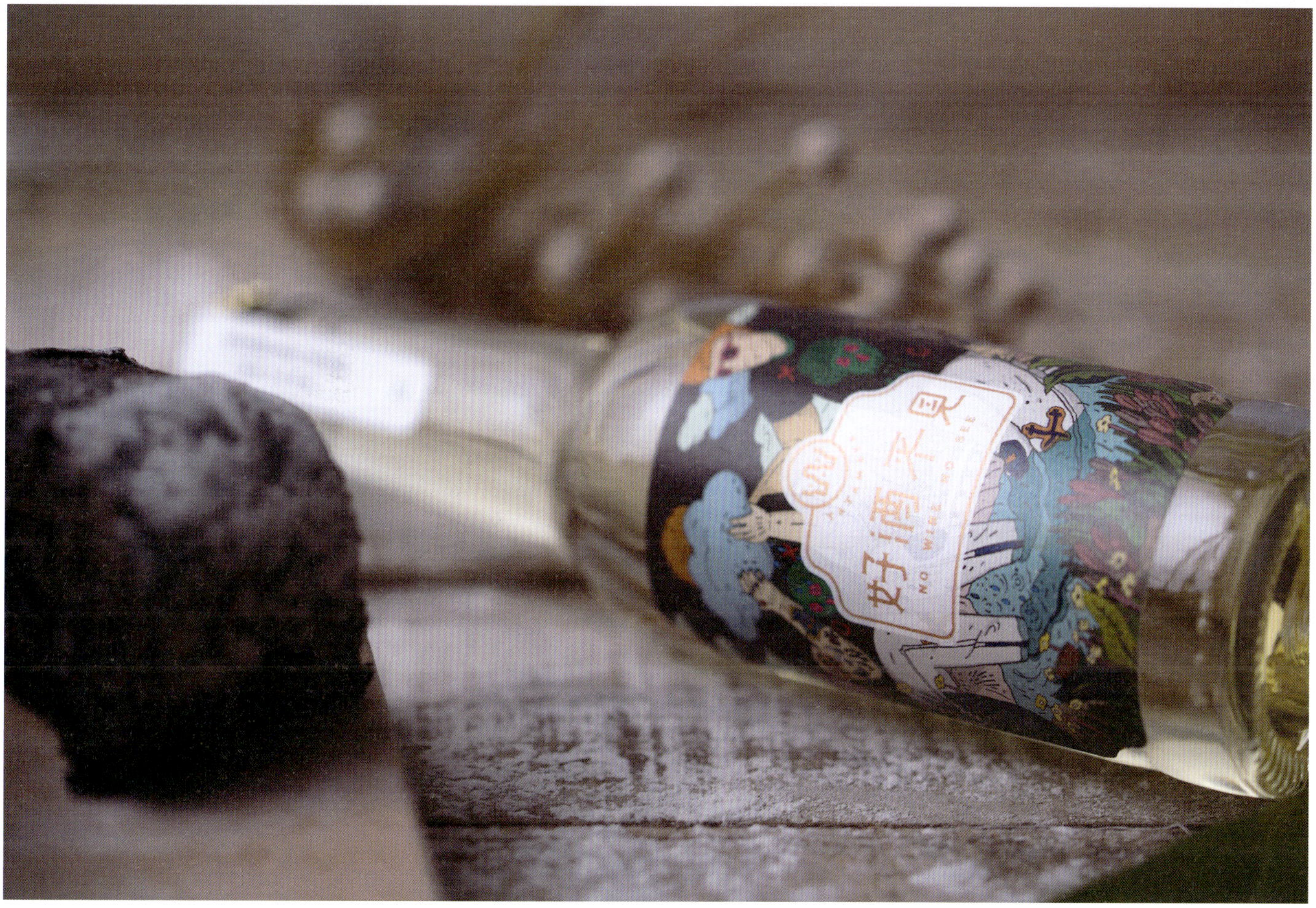
好酒不見

Prot Tea

Design FOX & OWL

Prot tea is a Taiwanese tea brand emphasizing the use of zisha teapots and authentic Taiwanese tea. The icon of a zisha teapot is therefore the key design element. The gold-embossed icon achieves stunning visual effect when applied to the black-and-blue boxes. Quality paper endows the embossing pattern with thickness and volume.

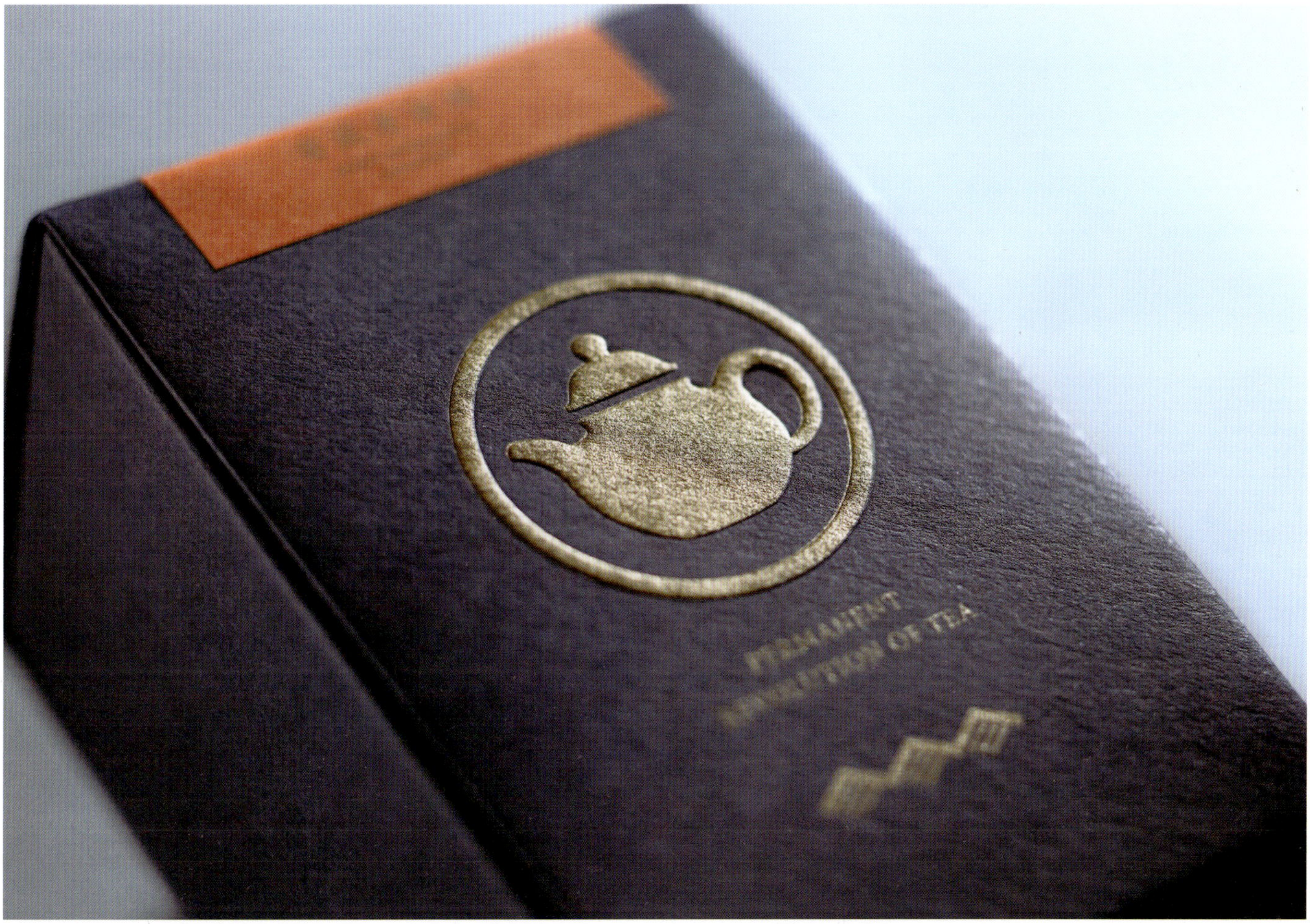
PERMANENT
REVOLUTION OF TEA

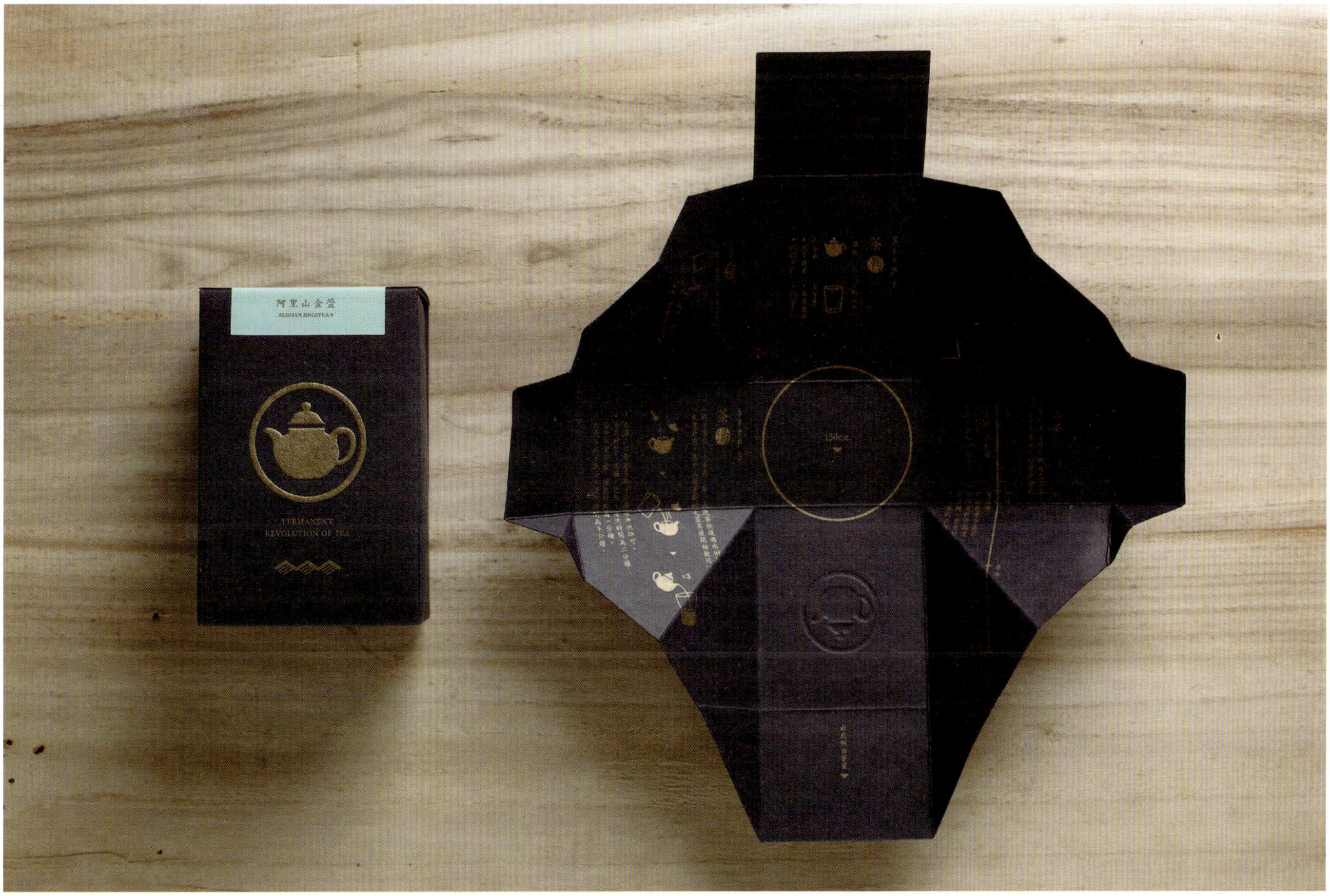

京盛宇
茶
京盛宇
茶
京盛宇
茶
京盛宇
白毫茉莉
JASMINE GREEN TEA
茶
100% TEA
特殊
風味
京盛宇
京盛宇
PERMANENT
REVOLUTION OF TEA

PERMANENT
REVOLUTION OF TEA
清香梨山烏龍
LISHAN OOLONG

Elegant Article in Sleeve, the Folding Fan of Suzhou

Design Jingren Lu

Elegant Article in Sleeve, the Folding Fan of Suzhou is a series of books thoroughly depicting the Suzhou folding fan (Suzhou being a city in China) designed during the Ming and Qing (1368 – 1911). To answer to this "ancient atmosphere," the covers for the series invoke tradition: using traditional thread as well as accordion bindings. The topics of the books are revealed via various icons of a fan. Silver-foil blocking is used to emphasize the icons while adding an elegant touch to the design.

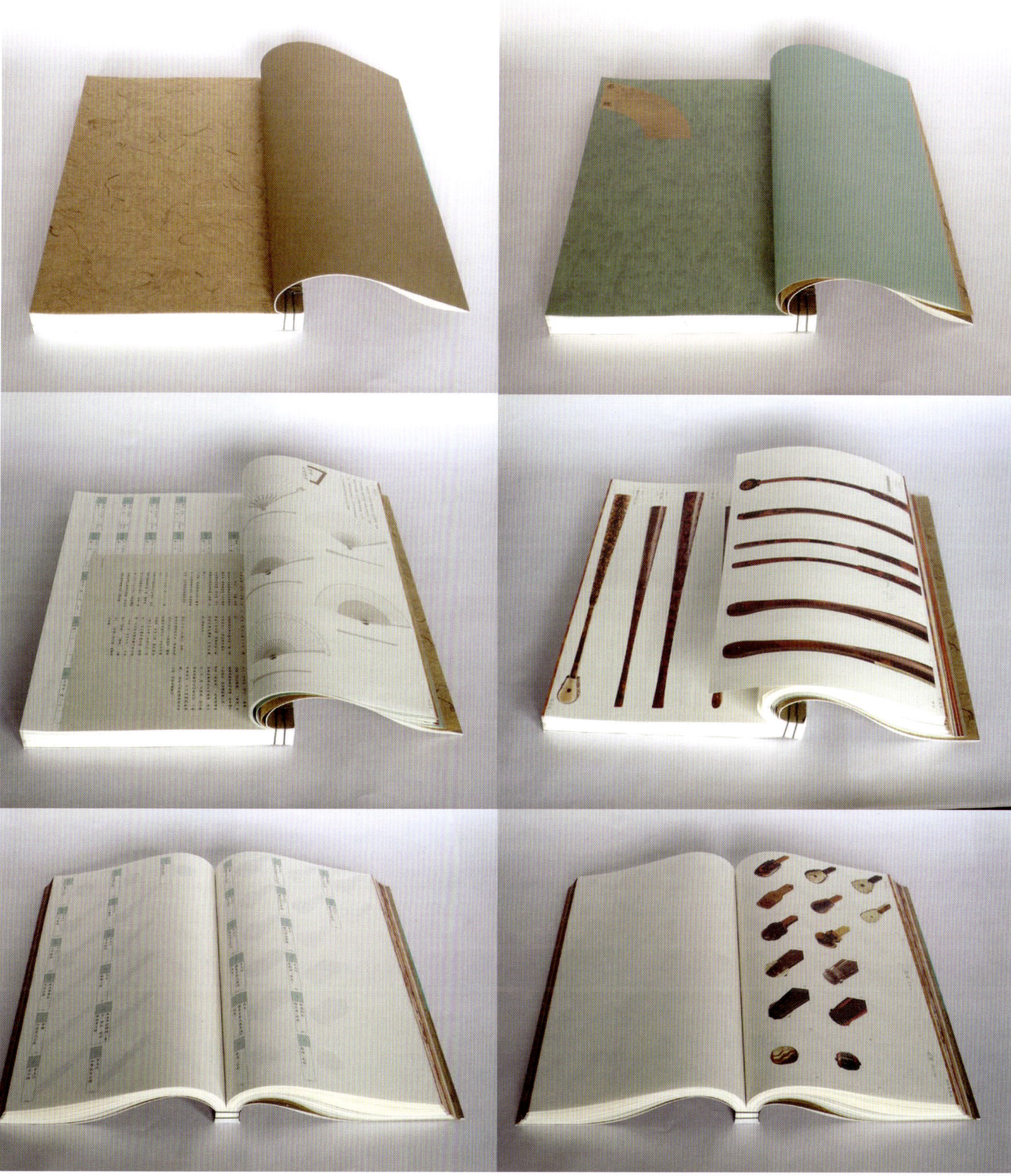

Bokeria Branding and Packaging

Design Anagrama

Bokeria is a restaurant known for serving high-quality dishes and a top wine selection, offering visitors an experience similar to being at home. Anagrama created an identity wherein the restaurant asserts its uniqueness. A typographic logo reflects the brand's modern and trendsetting culinary concept, while a series of stamps and gold elements complement and unify the variety of meats and flavors — an emphatic statement of quality and richness.

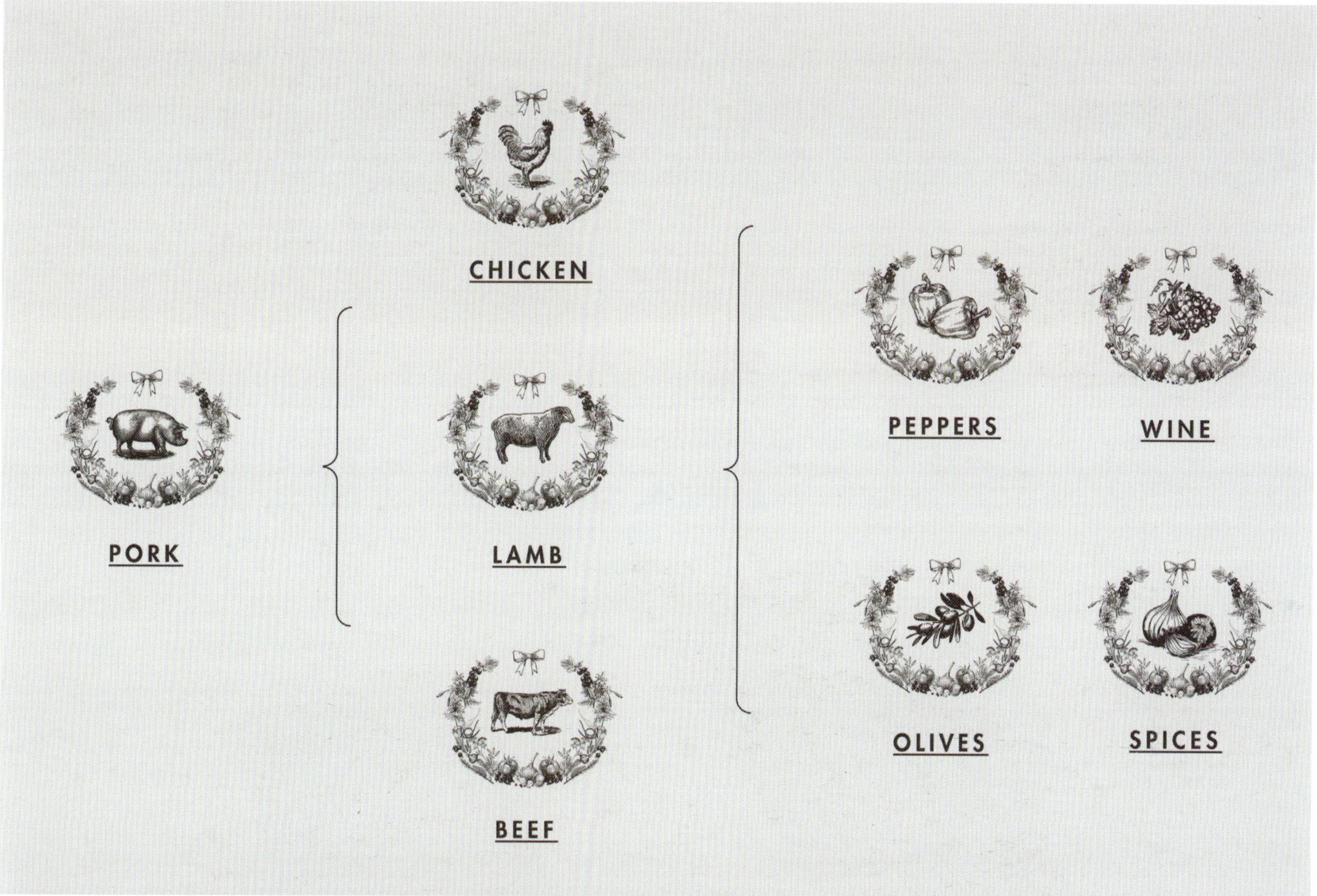

CHICKEN

PORK

LAMB

BEEF

PEPPERS

WINE

OLIVES

SPICES

Art Directors Club of New York Annual iPad Case

Design RM&CO

The Art Directors Club of New York (ADC) commissioned RM&CO to design a limited-edition iPad case to coincide with the first time in the ADC's 92-year history that no awards annual would be printed: a custom-made DODOcase to commemorate the launch of the ADC annual app. The handcrafted case is inspired by the classic Art Directors Annuals from the 1920s. On the front side of the case appears the organization's name, foil stamped. Embossed on the back is a medallion designed by sculptor Paul Manship in 1920 that honors the best creative work in the world. The foil embossing against the mat, black cover makes for a timeless design.

Foil Stamping

Mleko i Miód

Design BEZA PROJEKT S.C.

Mleko i Miód (Milk & Honey) is a set designed on behalf of the Ministry of Foreign Affairs for the Polish Presidency of the European Union. The set consists of a honey jar, a mug, a honey spoon, and a recipe necessary for preparing a drink deep-rooted in Polish tradition: milk and honey. The design is based on a minimalist concept unified by a golden element applied to all parts of the set, such as the edge of the mug, the raindrops, and the honeycomb pattern on the packaging. Infused with the natural color of honey, it creates a warm and noble atmosphere.

Robot Roy

Design Robot Food

For client Christmas gifts, Robot Food decided on a traditional wooden nutcracker with a robotic twist. The result is named Robot Roy the Nutcracker Toy. Fun, festive, and distinctly on brand, Robot Roy stands ten inches tall and is hand-painted in bright, primary colors. He's packaged in an impressive black box made from ebony Colorplan by GF Smith. The in-house illustrations include a festive nuts-and-bolts pattern, which decorates the box's edges. The design is applied in a luxurious, tactile gold foil finish, and the 50 limited-edition boxes are sealed with a numbered label.

ROBOT FOOD
ROBOT ROY
NUTCRACKER
Toy

RF
ROBOT FOOD
In creative we conquer.

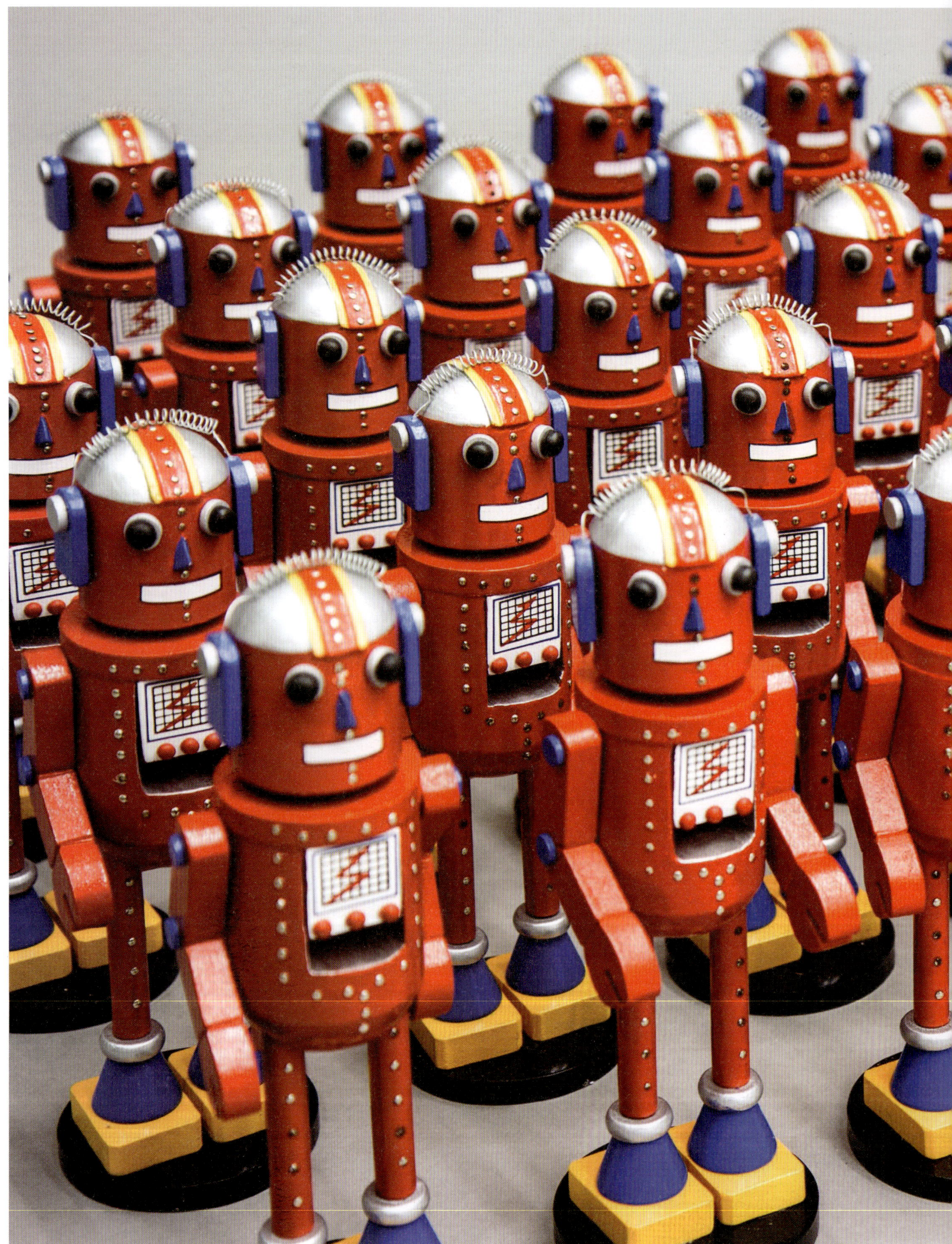

Bonne Année

Design Tramy Lui

This series of money packets is designed for France Macau Business Association Charity Gala Dinner. The money packets feature Macau and French landmarks, as well as mingle the two cultures with some typical elements. The illustration is printed in gold, with the golden lines providing a concise style.

BONNE ANNÉE!

BONNE ANNÉE!
BONNE ANNÉE!

FRANCE
EIFFEL TOWER
A SYMBOL OF FRENCH CULTURE. THE MAIN LANDMARK IN PARIS.
HOT AIR BALLNOON
IT ORIGINATED IN FRANCE. DEMONSTRATES THE IDENTITY, PERSONALITY, AND BRAVERY OF FRENCH.
MACAU TOWER
IT IS A FAMOUS LANDMARK IN MACAU, RANKING AS THE 21ST TALLEST FREE-STANDING TOWER IN THE WORLD.
LOTUS
IT IS THE FLORAL EMBLEM OF MACAU, WHICH SYMBOLISES PURITY, INTERGRITY

Brazilian Delights

Design New Greco

Embaré is one of the major companies in Brazil's food business. Its name means *tasty tree* in one indigenous tongue. The company's newly released Brazilian Delights line includes caramels of six typical Brazilian fruit flavors. The favors and their strong Brazilian nature are fully exploited in the packaging. Vivid images printed in a metallic green color against a yellow-varnished stock portray native legends about the fruits. The result is a fresh and modern caramel pack.

Palette Business Card

Design Kozlova Design

This business card was created for the young and very talented artist Elena Mirosedina. A Palette is an important tool for painter, and that is why the card is palette shaped, with a hole for attaching the card to products, as a label. Above the white information on the front side, her name is highlighted in red.

Julie Pop Bakery Cards

Design Bureau Rabensteiner

The Julie Pop Bakery makes cake pops. By featuring various metallic hues, the business card reflects the colorful variety of handmade cake pops. Bright colors perk up the cards just as the cake pops' deliciousness and artful presentation make them stand out.

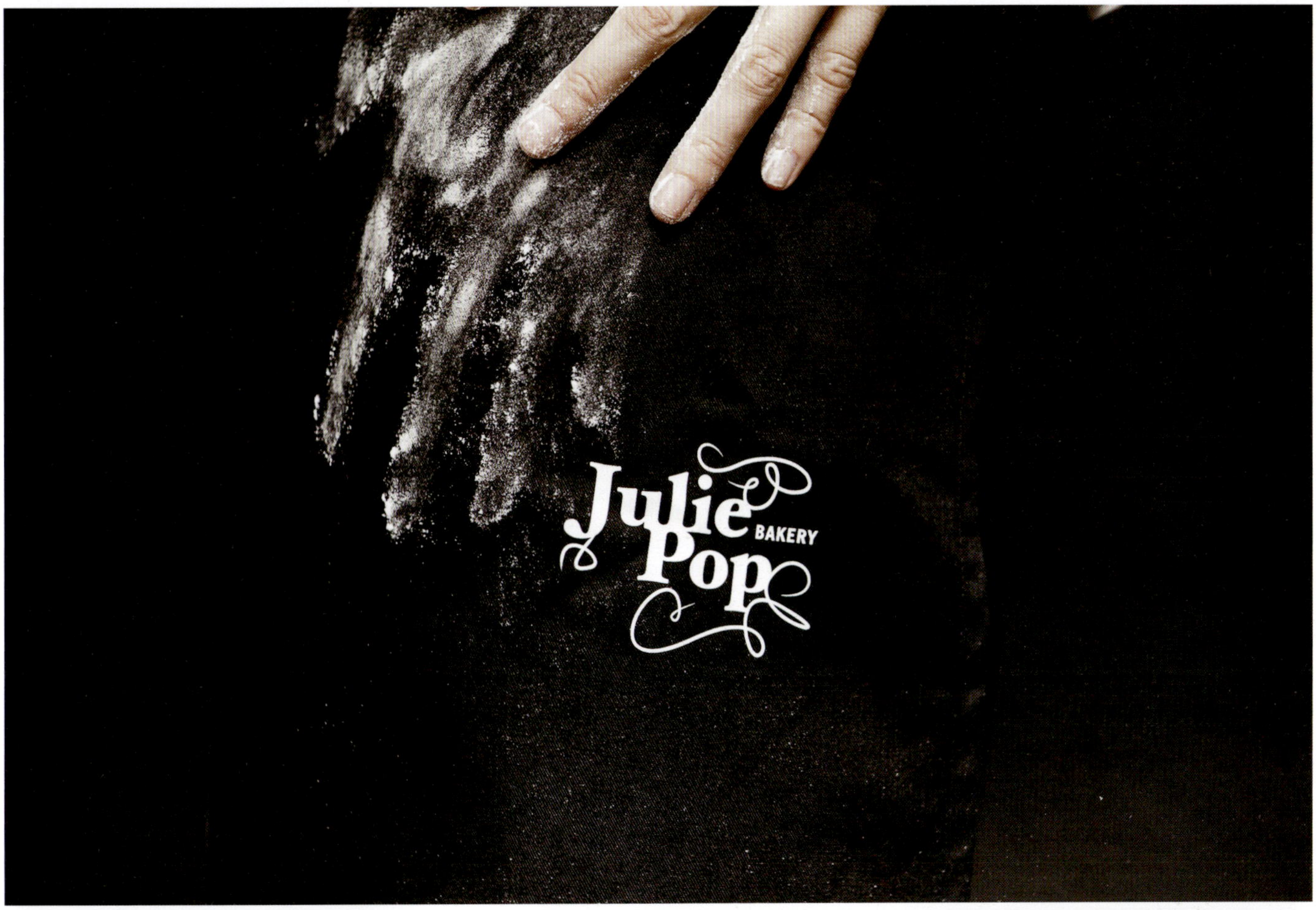
Julie Pop
BAKERY

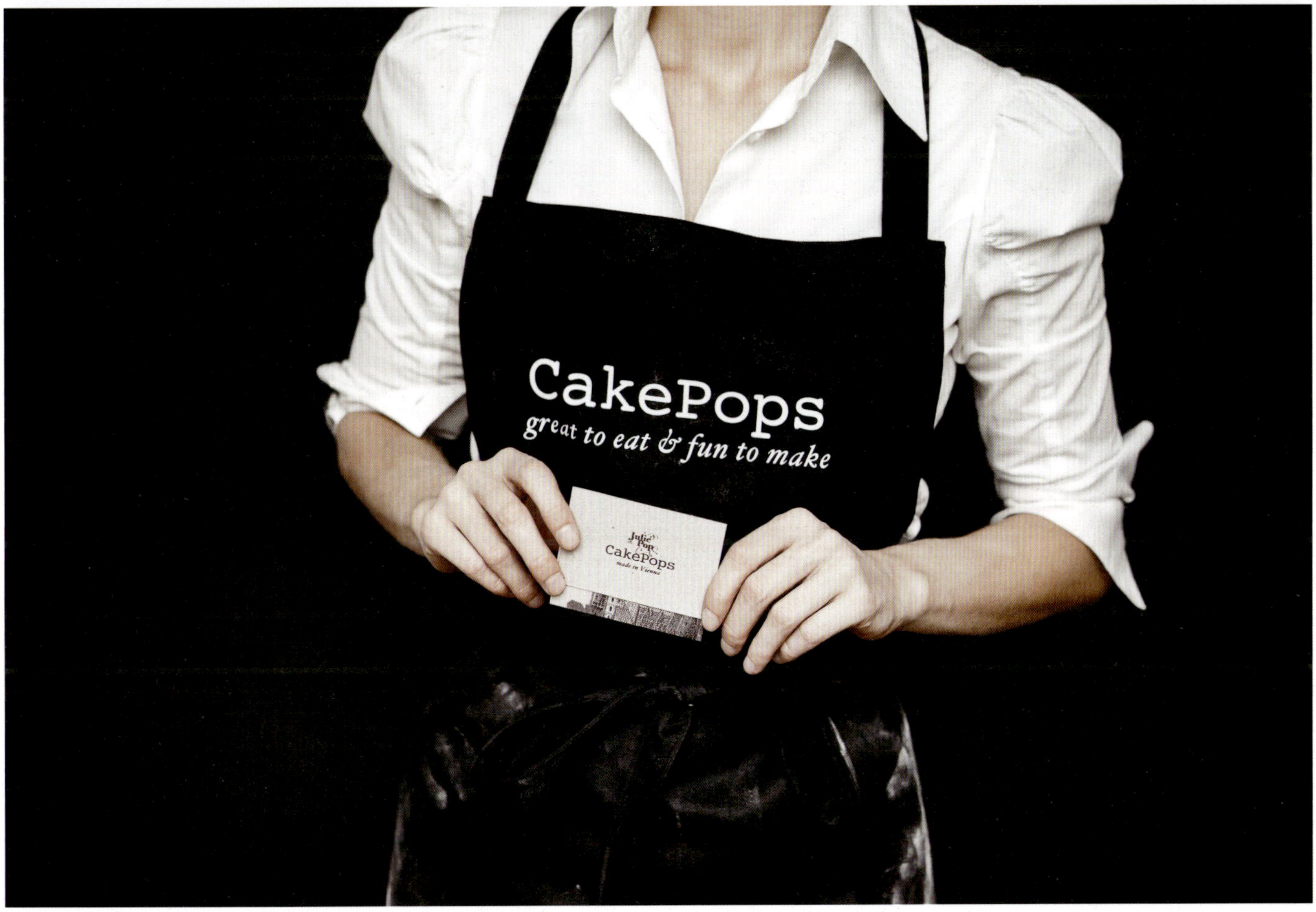
CakePops
great to eat & fun to make

Warmth of Sunshine

Design MURA Design

This packaging is for a souvenir from Taiwan. Designed around the concept of traveling memories, the illustration on the packaging portrays a pastoral landscape alluding to the wonderful moments travelers experience in Taiwan. The pastel tones provide a perfectly fit for the countryside scenery, and the moderately metallic logotype and souvenir name add subtleness and quality to the whole presentation.

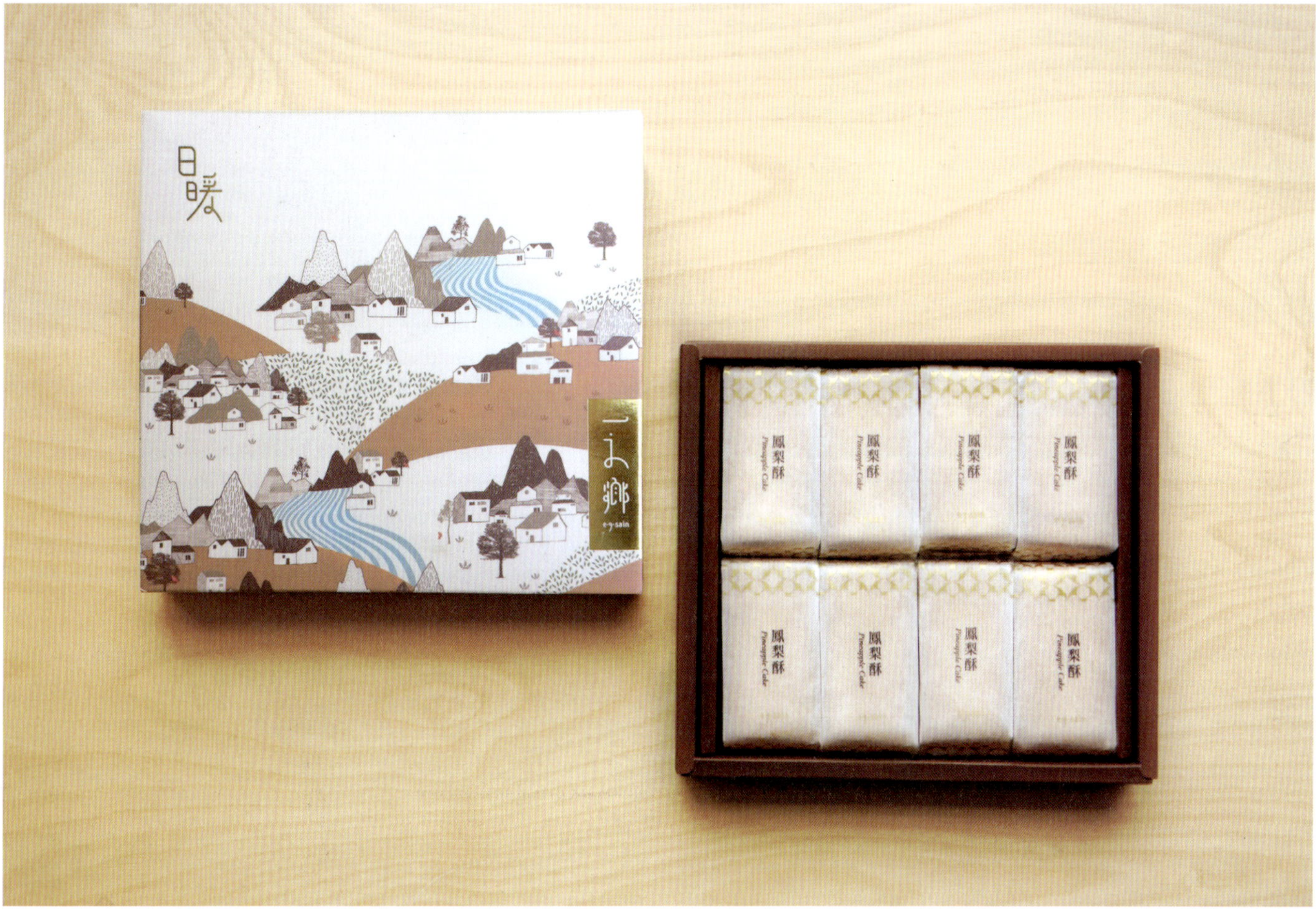
日暖
鳳梨酥
Pineapple Cake

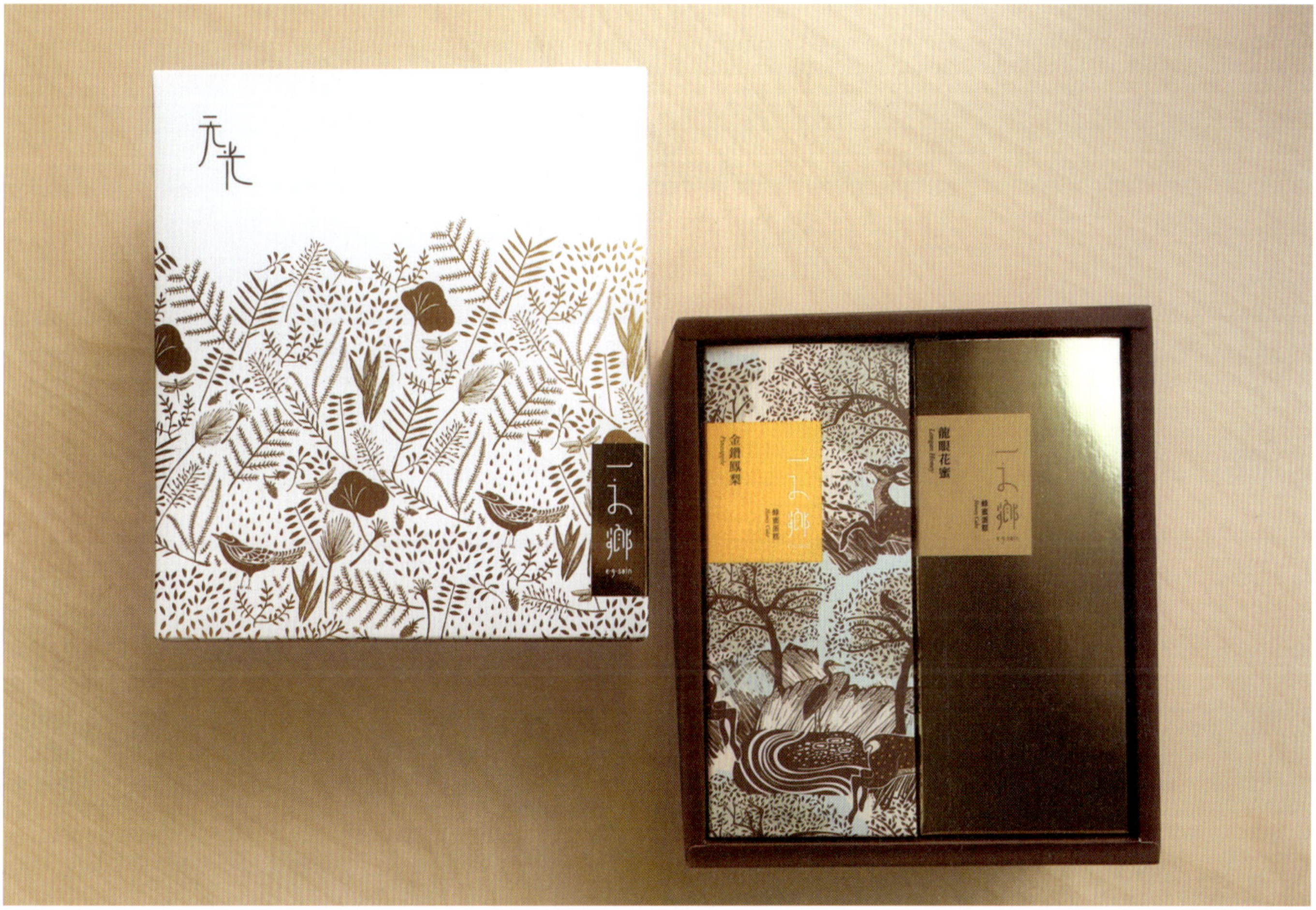
金鑽鳳梨
龍眼花蜜

Goji Serum Pack

Design So Cool Design Office

Goji Serum is an innovative Greek facial care product. Its beneficial properties make it a golden purchasing choice. This newly improved formula has been released in Russian market since the beginning of 2015. The version's updated packaging shines like a jewel that any woman would want to possess. The designers, therefore, selected gold lettering on superfine paper, with a special pattern of goji berry and unconventional triangular shape. The glittering gold color exudes an air of opulence.

BIO
GojiSerum
THE ELIXIR OF BEAUTY
GREEK ORGANIC PRODUCT
DERMATOLOGICALLY TESTED
gojiBEAUTÉ
BIO
GojiSerum
THE ELIXIR OF BEAUTY
GREEK ORGANIC PRODUCT
DERMATOLOGICALLY TESTED
gojiBEAUTÉ

Got One!! Wild Mullet Catch

Design Devours Restaurant STUDIO

This packaging was designed to convey the joy of capturing a mullet fish in wild nature. Its exterior is a fishing net, which contains the product's box. On the solid-black box is embossed a golden mullet. The color palette of black-gold not only responds to mullet 's alternative name, *black gold*, it also creates a premium touch. Accenting environmental protection, all the materials are either recycled or upcycled.

捕獲!!

Oddds the New Anthropology

Design Oddds

Oddds' rebranding is conveyed with new stationery ranging from name cards, envelopes, postcards, thank-you cards, and tags to packaging. With crafted finishing, each is typographically driven and executed with the careful detailing that epitomizes the new Oddds. The logotype, printed with gold foil arranged impressively, stands out against the jet-black paper, creating a mood of secrecy.
Materials and simplicity are expressed through the craft of letterpress, matt gold, and copper foils.

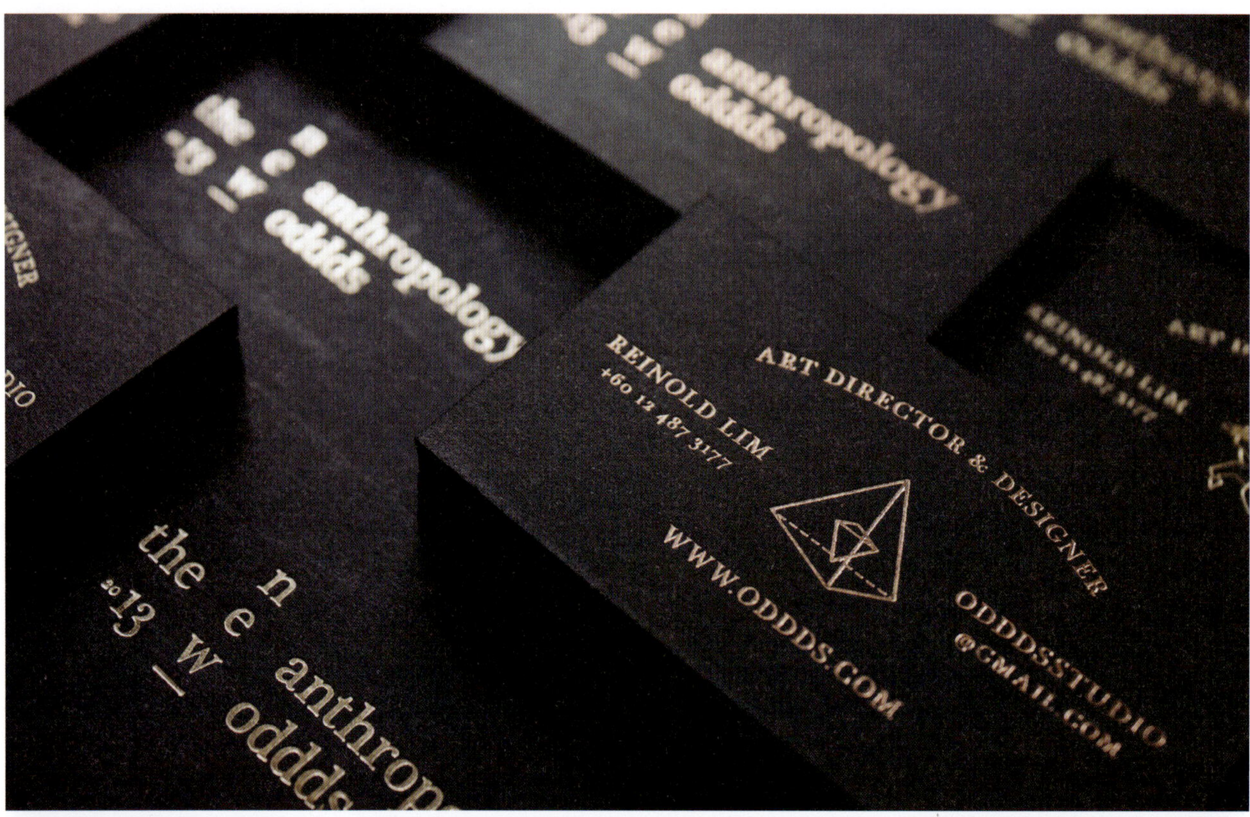

the new anthropology
2013 oddds
HUMBLY SEALED, PACKED
& HANDLED BY ODDDS
WWW.ODDDS.COM
RECIPIENT
ALL GOODS WERE HANDSOMELY MADE
WITH INTENTIONS & ACCURACY

THE NEW ANTHROPOLOGY BY ODDDS
UNLIMITED VISIBLE LANGUAGE
A CERTAIN MYSTIQUE IN FUTURISM

A LITTLE FORM OF
GRATITUDE TO
the n e w anthropology
odds
DESIGN DIRECTOR & DESIGNER
SARAH TAN
ODDDSSTUDIO
@GMAIL.COM
The NEW Anthropology
BY ODDDS
BRAVERY in HUNTING
THAT BRINGS TOGETHER
The NEW Anthropology
BY ODDDS

ODDDS
the new
anthropology
ODDDS

Happy Goat (Gold) Year

Design EBS Design

For the Chinese Year of Goat (2015), EBS combined the shapes of the Chinese characters 羊 (goat) and 年 (year) on their New Year's gift package for clients. The new literary image applied on the red money packet is printed in gold to make a pun between the *goat* and *gold* characters. The design then decomposes and re-arranges the characters' strokes, also in gold. The design expresses best wishes.

Nimb Boutique Hotel

Design homework

Nimb is a boutique hotel in Copenhagen. Obsessed with quality and provenance, its identity system depends on the most fundamental of colors — black information on white paper. Thus, when the logotype Nimb is processed with a silver finish and applied to various elements of the system, it becomes a focus of attention, as well as generating a stylish modern impression.

Nimb

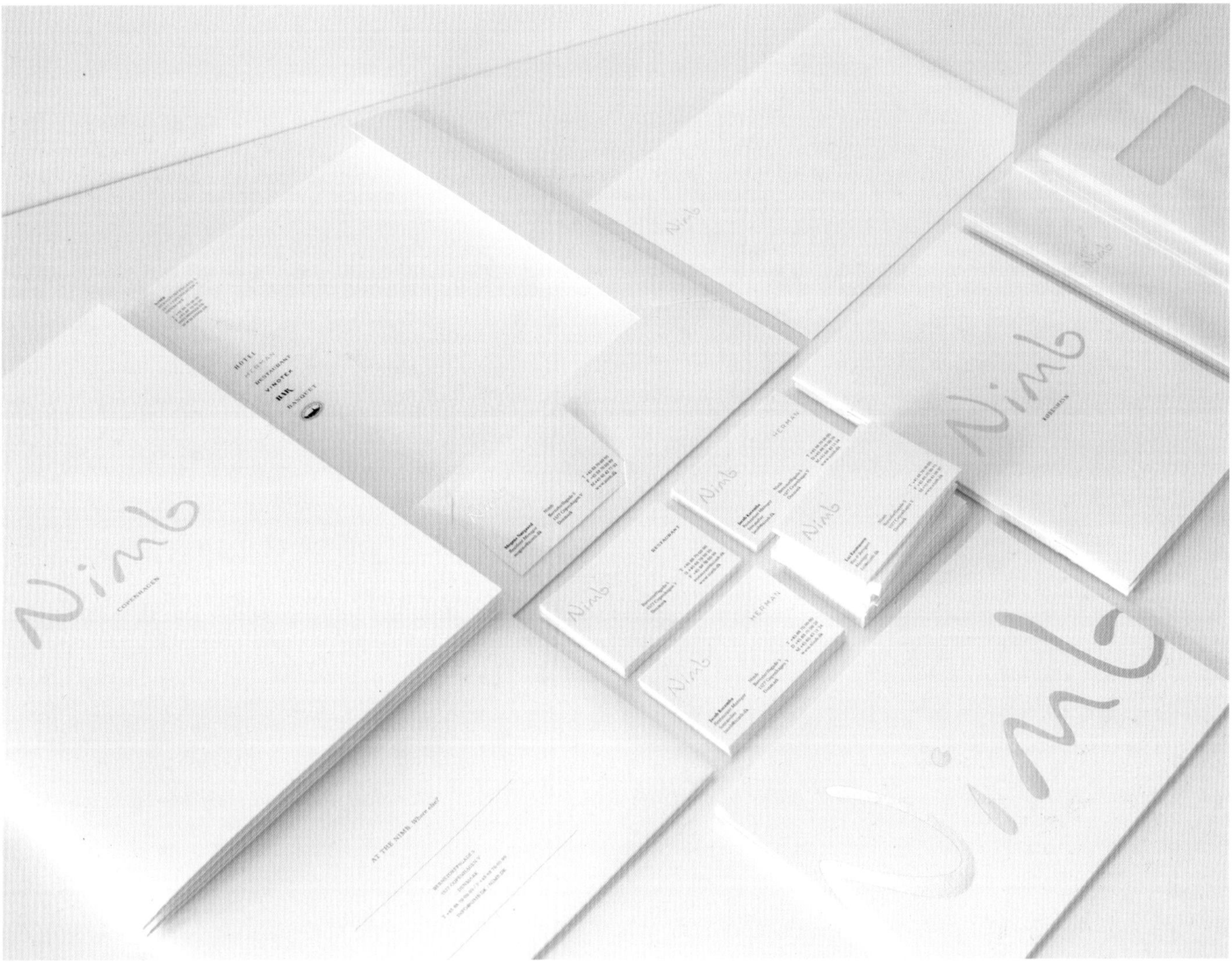

The 48th Golden Camera from HÖRZU

Design Paperlux GmbH

For the 48th awards presentation of the Golden Camera from HÖRZU, Paperlux designed a suite of communication materials centered around an exclusively made font. The typeface is composed of geometric shapes and fine lines that render an elegant and contemporary feel further emphasized by the use of gold foils. The selected gray paper, refined with iriodin lacquer finishing, is also a vital element of the design, creating a subtle and elegant event atmosphere together with the luminous fonts.

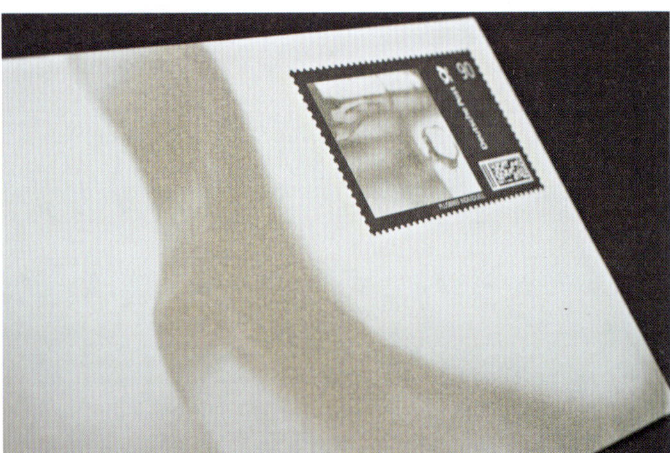

DIE
48.
GØLD
ENE
KAM
ERA
VON HÖRZU
SCHR
EIBEN
SIE
UNS
ZU
RÜCK
HÖRZU, BITTEN WIR
ZUR 48. VERLEIHUNG

SCHÖNE
GRÜSSE
UND
SCHÖNE
MO
MENTE
HOTEL
INFORMA
TION

Jealous Sweets

Design B&B studio

Jealous Sweets is a gelatin and gluten-free confectionery line that needed updated packaging to communicate the brand's premium positioning and a gift worthiness. B&B studio first linked the brand name back to the sweets themselves via the idea of covetable candy — a concept illustrated by a precious-jewel icon and an imposing magpie with an eye for something special. The studio also designs boxes comprising a die-cut sleeve featuring glossing, embossing and foil blocking: all secured by a gold foil tamper seal atop a patterned lift-lid box. The details add up to desirable and luxurious boxes for an extra special experience.

JEALOUS
Sweets
CURIOUSLY
COVETABLE CANDY
CRAZY GUMS
Irresistibly Yummy Sweets

JEALOUS
Sweets
SOUR BEANS
SWEET REVOLUTION
Notoriously Tasty Sweets
CRAZY GUMS
Irresistibly Yummy Sweets

JEALOUS
Sweets
CURIOUSLY
COVETABLE CANDY
JEALOUS
Sweets
GUMMY BEARS
JEALOUS
Sweets
CURIOUSLY
COVETABLE CANDY
JEALOUS
Sweets
CURIOUSLY
COVETABLE CANDY

Maderista

Design Anagrama

Maderista is a carpentry boutique offering custom-made furniture sourced only from the finest woods. Anagrama created two icons for its logo: a bear and a nail. The bear embodies the natural strength and robustness of wood, Maderista's primary material, whereas the nail exemplifies the skilled craftsmanship and attention put into each commissioned piece of furniture. The paper for the stationery is porous and off-white: crafty, yet with touches of hot-stamped gold conveying the craftsmanship of the brand while embracing its high-end quality and class.

MADERISTA
EST 1979
SAB 11:00 AM A 7.00 PM
81.8335.3412 / 81.8335.1516
WWW.MADERISTA.MX

MADERISTA
EST 1979
LUCILA ZAMORA

MADERISTA
EST 1979
EBANISTAS

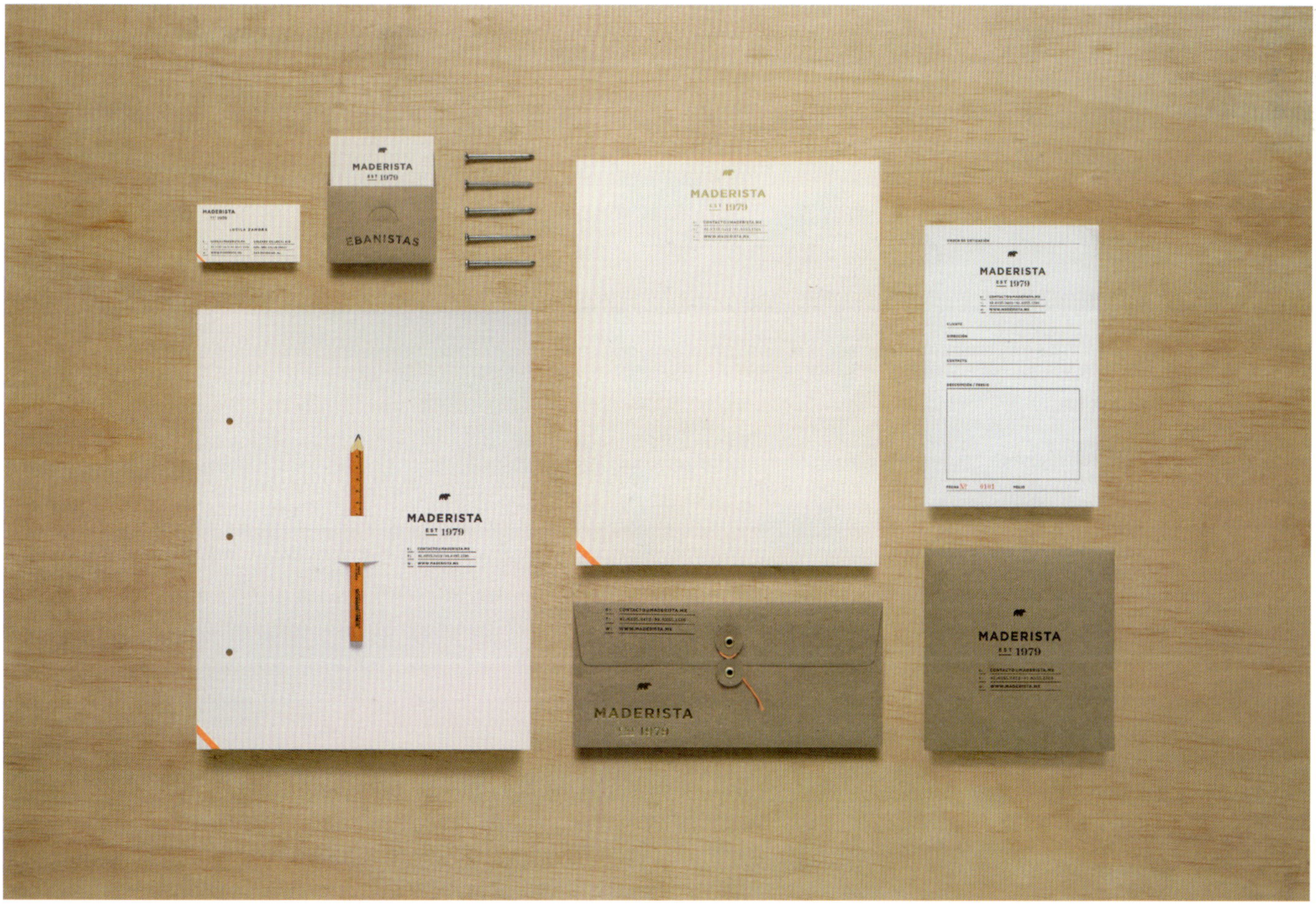

Marble Cakery Identity

Design José Jiménez Lara

Marble Cakery is a concept designed for a popular pastry chef, whose most famous recipe is Blueberry White-Chocolate Cake.
The naming and patterns refer to marble cakes, recipes that use two different doughs in the same cake, yielding a marbling effect in each slice. The logo is an *m* (for marble), representing the typical mold used for the cakes. Its shape adapts to the size of the cake: big, medium, or one portion. The gold effect of the logo and the edges of the stationary complete the identity and lend a delicate appearance.

The Miracle of the Golden Pearl

Design Milan Janic

The Miracle of the Golden Pearl is a book created for Jewelmer, the leading golden pearl farmer (of pearls that are naturally golden) in the Philippines. The book was offset printed, with gold as a fifth color. A select UV varnish overprint was used on the golden pages for maps of the over 7,000 Philippines islands. The hard cover was padded with golden embossing and golden gilt edge. Echoing the golden pearl, the golden visual effect of the book is an emphatic statement of the pearl's preciousness and opulence.

miracle
de la perle
Didier Brodbeck
the miracle

le miracle
de la perle d'o
miracle

le miracle de la perle d'or · the miracle of th

Mild Whistle Identity

Design Oddds

This funky visual identity, based on stylish letterpress effects, is designed for Singapore designer Mild Whistle. The custom-made logotype and illustrated icons in rose-gold foiling work with a soft turquoise for contrast, yielding a modern design.

MILD WHISTLE
ART DIRECTION & DESIGN
MILDWHISTLE@GMAIL.COM

Soul Archive

Design Rice Creative

The packaging for these photographic art prints, *Soul Archive*, is fashioned from solid-black, thick, foldable paper. When the "cover" is folded into a "box" and rests on a book shelf, the design looks like a book. All the information inside and outside the "cover" is gold-foil stamped. The black-gold color palette grounds a classic aesthetic and timeless statement.

SOUL ARCHIVE
1
NOW IN VIET-NAM

SOUL ARCHIVE

Tabarka Branding

Design Anagrama

Anagrama designed a slick new identity for terracotta tile manufacturer Tabarka Studio.
The concept came from Tabarka's intricate hand-crafted tiles for its logo design and then was extracted as a blue-and-silver scale pattern across the branding. All the pieces tend to be classic and simple, such as the limited color palette, the tile icon and the subtle foil-stamped element. Meanwhile, they are reminiscent of the brand offering.

TABARKA
STUDIO

Chin Chin

Design Project of Imagination (POI)

The name card of Chin Chin's (a Melbourne-based Asian cuisine restaurant) basement bar, Go Go, is made out of black, tactile paper on which a tongue-in-cheek logo and the information glitter. The simple design and material bring to mind a sultry bar.

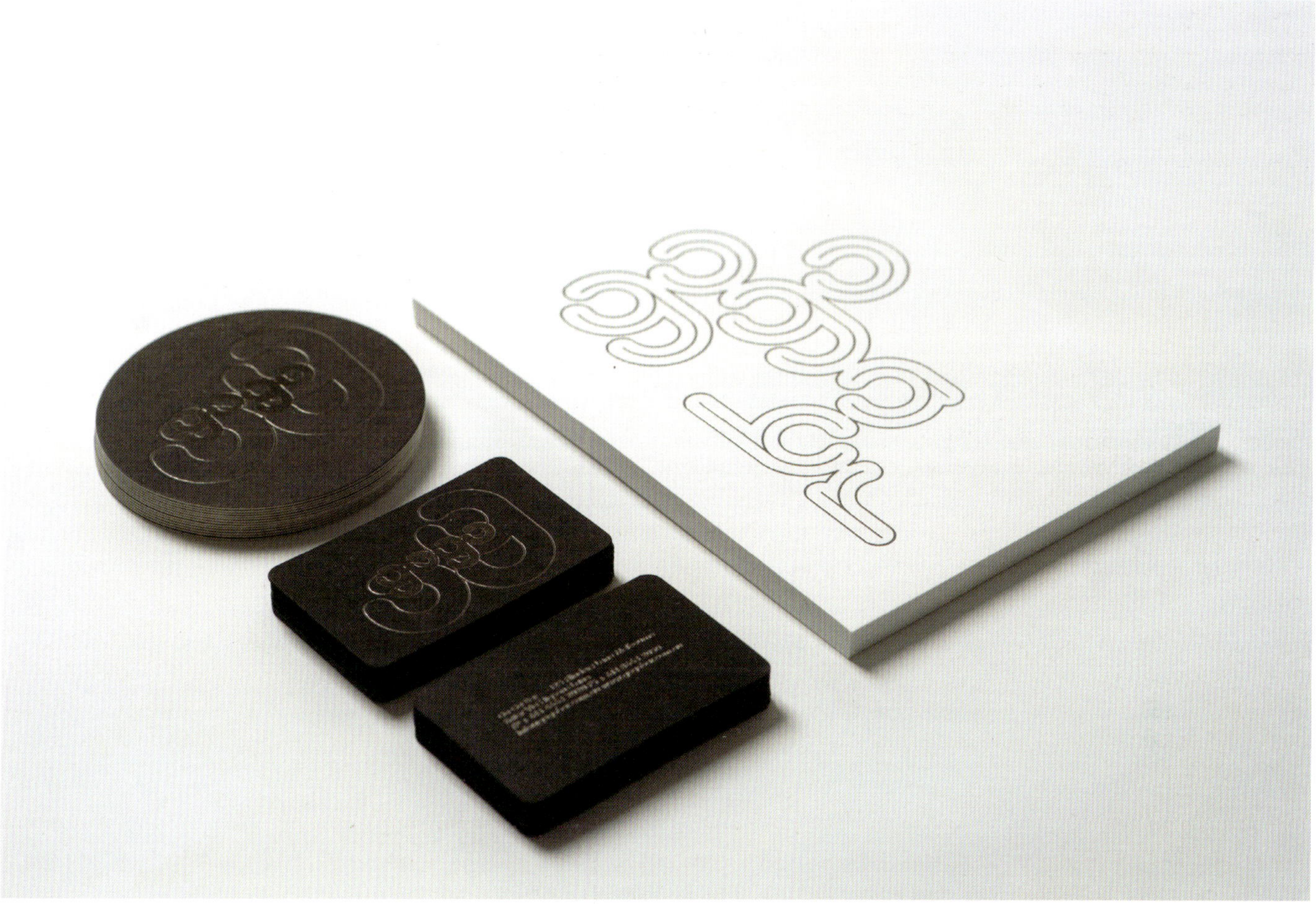

CHINCHIN
125 FLINDERS LANE MELBOURNE V A 2000
CHINCHIN
CHINCHIN
DJ HAPPY CHOW
& SPECIAL GUESTS
8PM - ONWARDS
MUSIC & FOOD
125 FLINDERS LNE.

Hotel Minho

Hotel Minho is located in Vila Nova de Cerveira, north of Portugal. Its renewed image, inspired by Theo van Doesburg's (1883–1931) designs, features a new logo in geometric typeface. The identity also makes use of a stag (the symbol of the region), in varying positions, to offer a more compelling result. Such details as changing colors, blind embossing, and foil application add variation to the whole design.

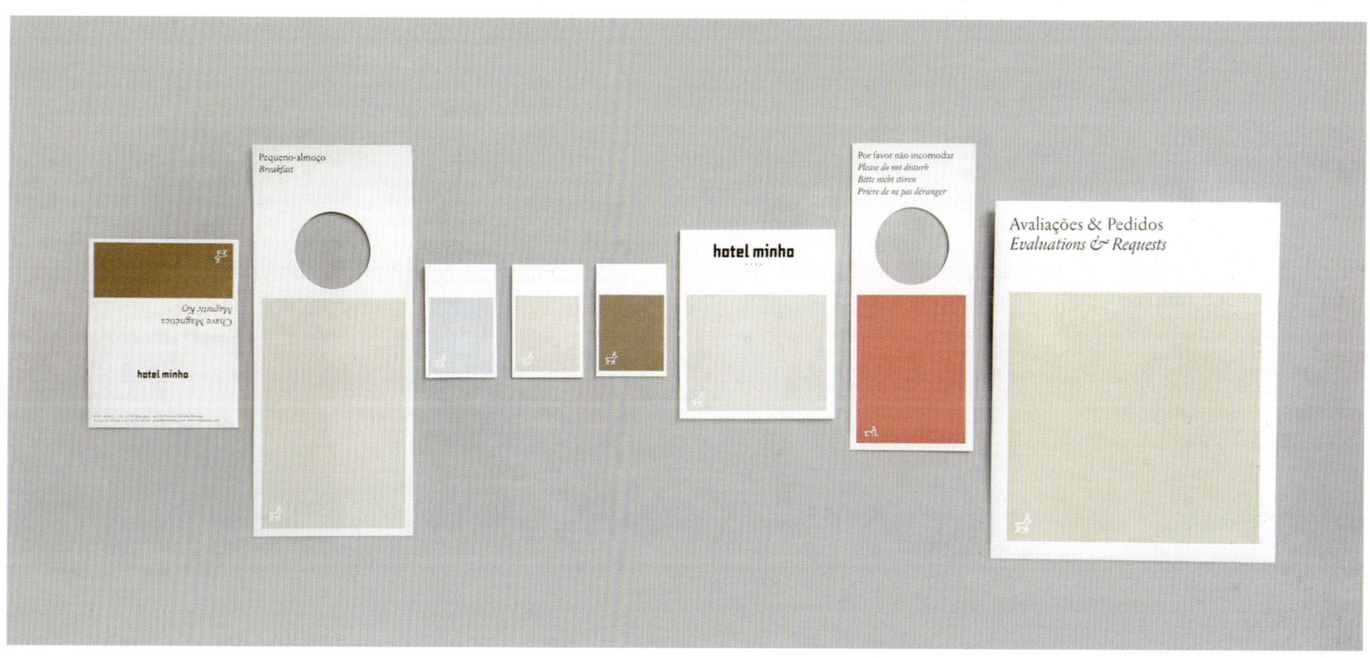
Pequeno-almoço
Breakfast
Chave Magnética
Magnetic Key
hotel minho
hotel minho
Por favor não incomodar
Please do not disturb
Bitte nicht stören
Prière de ne pas déranger
Avaliações & Pedidos
Evaluations & Requests

Tischlerei Gebrüder Falgschlunger

Design Bureau Rabensteiner

This is the corporate identity for Tischlerei Gebrüder Falgschlunger, a family-run Austrian carpentry company since 1929. The minimalist identity refines the look and feel of the brand with a focus on their exemplary ability to balance their woodworking tradition with a modern touch.

From the wood brown of the business card, binders, and tiny envelope, to the gold leaf logo, every piece evokes the nature-based quality of old world carpentry. The details, such as the foil finishing and letterpress effect, exemplify the brand's emphasis on quality. The bright neon green as a contrasting element adds a modern touch.

TISCHLER
STAMMTISCH

Turnstyle Business Papers

Design Turnstyle

Turnstyle's stationery system is simple, sparse, and beautiful in its use of negative space and color. Black and white letterpress on natural-colored, uncoated, art paper grounds the materials in traditional stationery aesthetics. Gilded gold edges complimented by gold-foil stamps elsewhere in the business cabinet augment the luxury and sophistication. Bright-red foil slashes corresponding to the diagonals in the *R* and *N* of the logo on the opposite side of the card, interact against the contact information in defiance of traditional norms of custom and legibility. These intrusive strokes act as "cross-outs," negating all but the one bit of contact information that is really necessary in our digital world — the e-mail address.

TURNSTYLE
4743 BALLARD AVENUE NW NUMBER 200
SEATTLE WASHINGTON 98107
TURNSTYLESTUDIO.COM
TO:

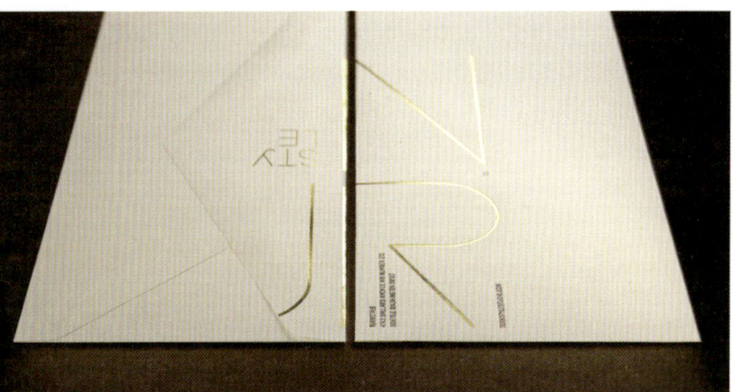

TURNSTYLE
4743 BALLARD AVENUE NW NUMBER 200
SEATTLE WASHINGTON 98107
TURNSTYLESTUDIO.COM
TO:

Red Packet Design

Design Shenzhen Pure Life Trading Co.,Ltd

Named *good news*, this series of red packet uses eight traditional kinds of auspicious Chinese symbols, such as phoenix, swallow, and mandarin duck, as the main elements for the set design. Each packet is designed around one of the visual symbols while the box for the packets collects all the symbols, fusing them into the Chinese character 囍(double happiness). The images are processed with either silver foil or gold foil. The finishing adds a tactile feeling, as well as enriching a sumptuous visual effect within the rich color palette.

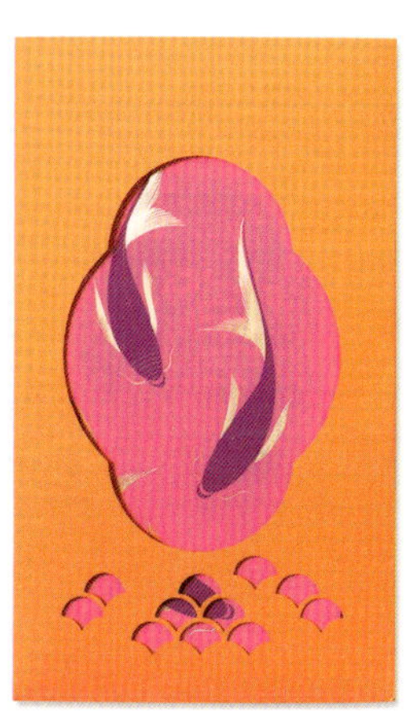
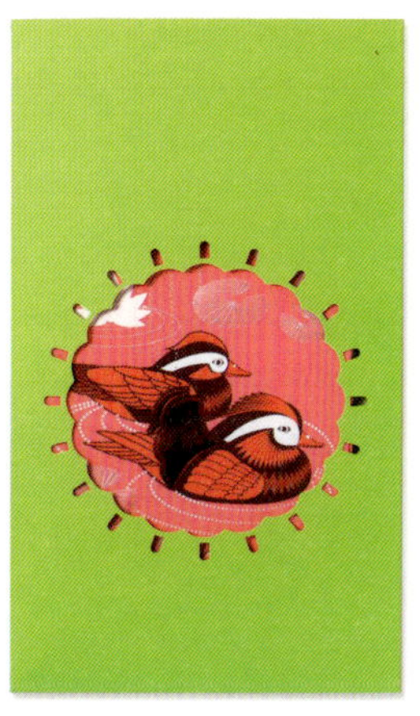

Embossing and Debossing

Mimicking sculptural relief art, embossing and debossing are two frequently used techniques for creating either raised or recessed images in paper and other substrates. Images and patterns thus created extend in various degrees either above or below the background. This results in the so-called relief effect, which enhances the product's artistic appeal.

How It Works

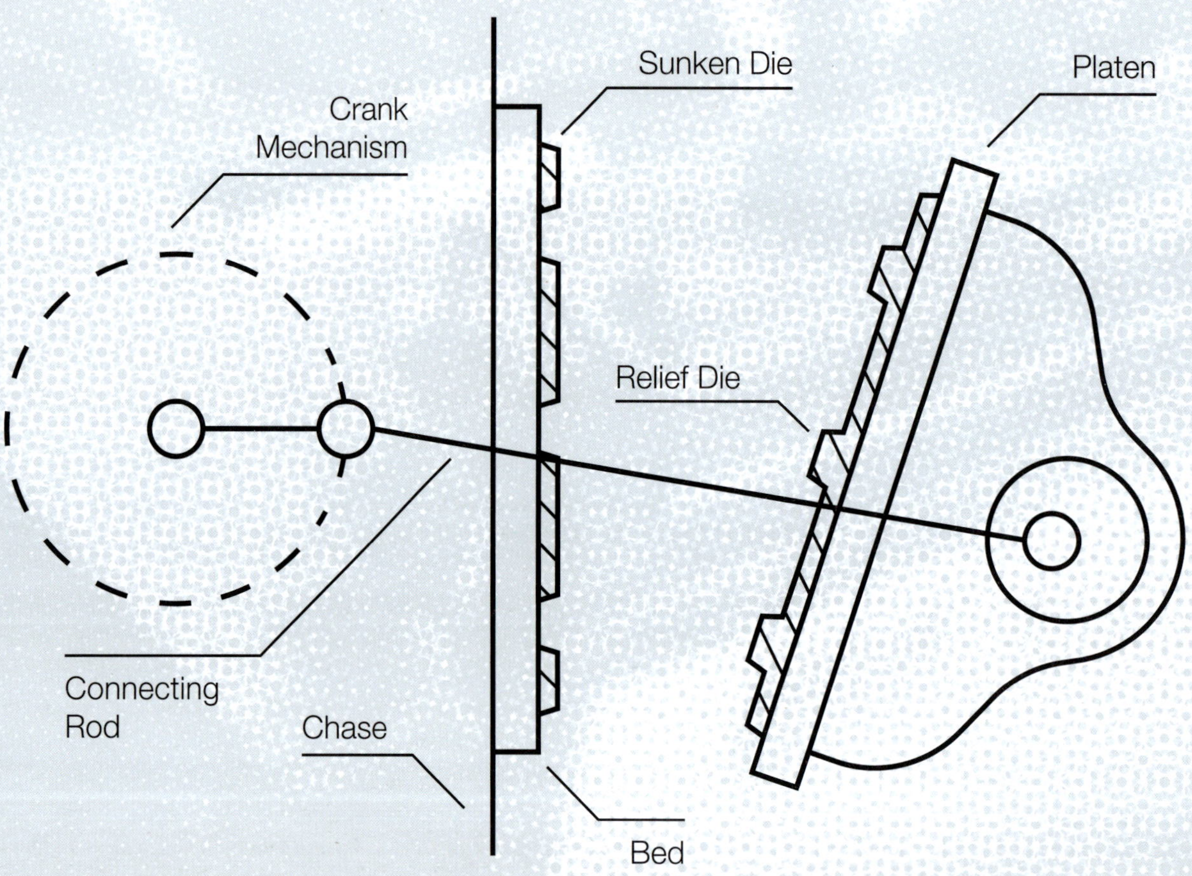

Embossing and Debossing Press Illustration

In practice, both embossing and debossing require an etched metal (female) die and a matching (male) counter die. Between the two is placed the substrate to be squeezed by the dies. When pressure is applied to the dies, a three-dimensional effect appears on the paper. When the pressure is applied from the back side of the paper, forcing the surface to rise, it is called *embossing*. When pressure is applied from the front side, creating an indented pattern, it is called *debossing*.

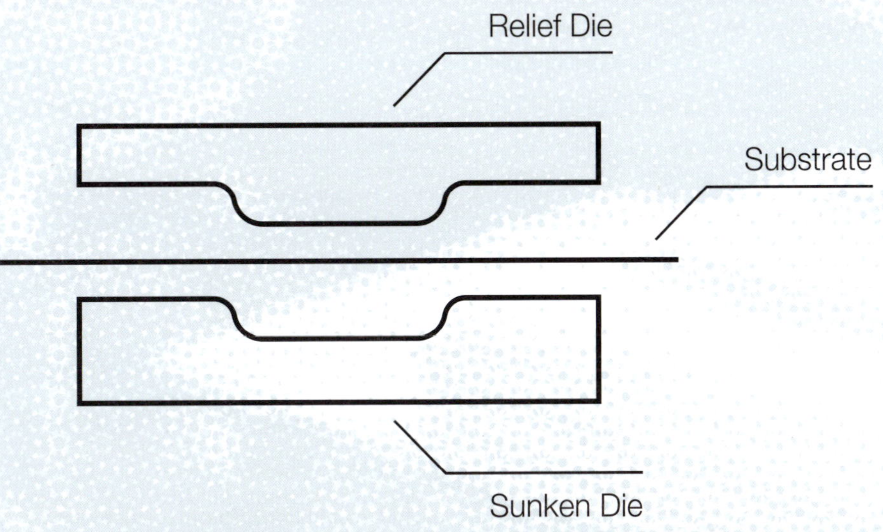

Sketch Map of Embossing and Debossing

View From Right of Manual Embossing and Debossing Press

The Crank Mechanism of Manual Embossing and Debossing Press

Embossing and debossing are eco-friendly and easy: offering two commercial printing techniques widely applied to many substrates, especially paper stock used for books, cards, and packaging.

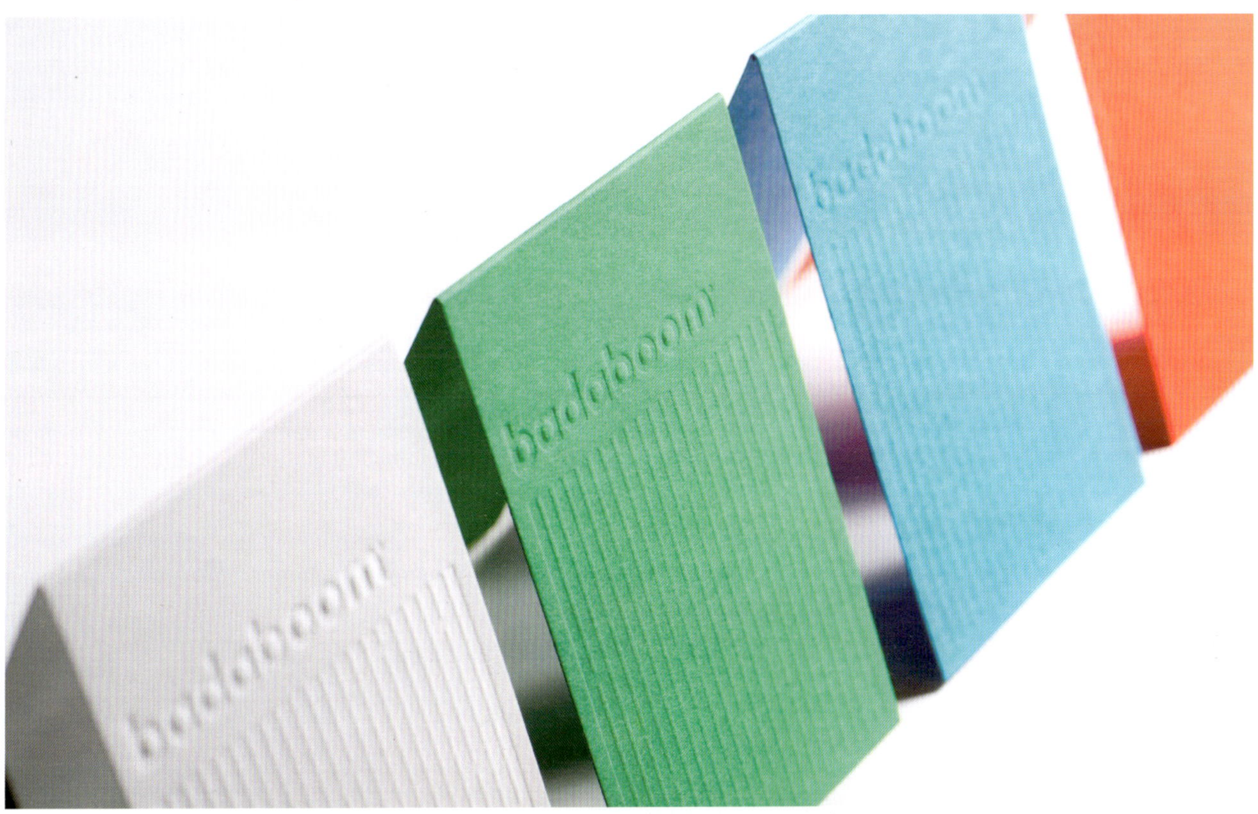
badaboom
badaboom
badaboom
badaboom

Erik
Modig
EFFEKTIV

Though it is easy to emboss or deboss, emphasis should be placed on the choice of paper and die — two elements of vital importance to the quality of the final product.

Die

The metals most often used for die construction are zinc, magnesium, copper, and brass.

Zinc is a soft, nondurable metal often used on small runs.

The hardness of magnesium is between that of zinc and copper. So magnesium die is relatively more durable than zinc die. It is a good choice for printing fine lines.

Copper die is stronger than magnesium die and lasts for far more impressions. Etching in this metal is able to generate fine images for a demanding emboss or deboss.

Brass is a superior metal alloy for quality, durable dies. It is much harder, which makes it better for crisp, medium-to-fine detail in medium-to-long print runs. It also offers favorable heat transfer and retention properties.

Embossing and Debossing Die Set

Embossing and Debossing Die Set

Relief Die / Male Die

Sunken Die / Female Die

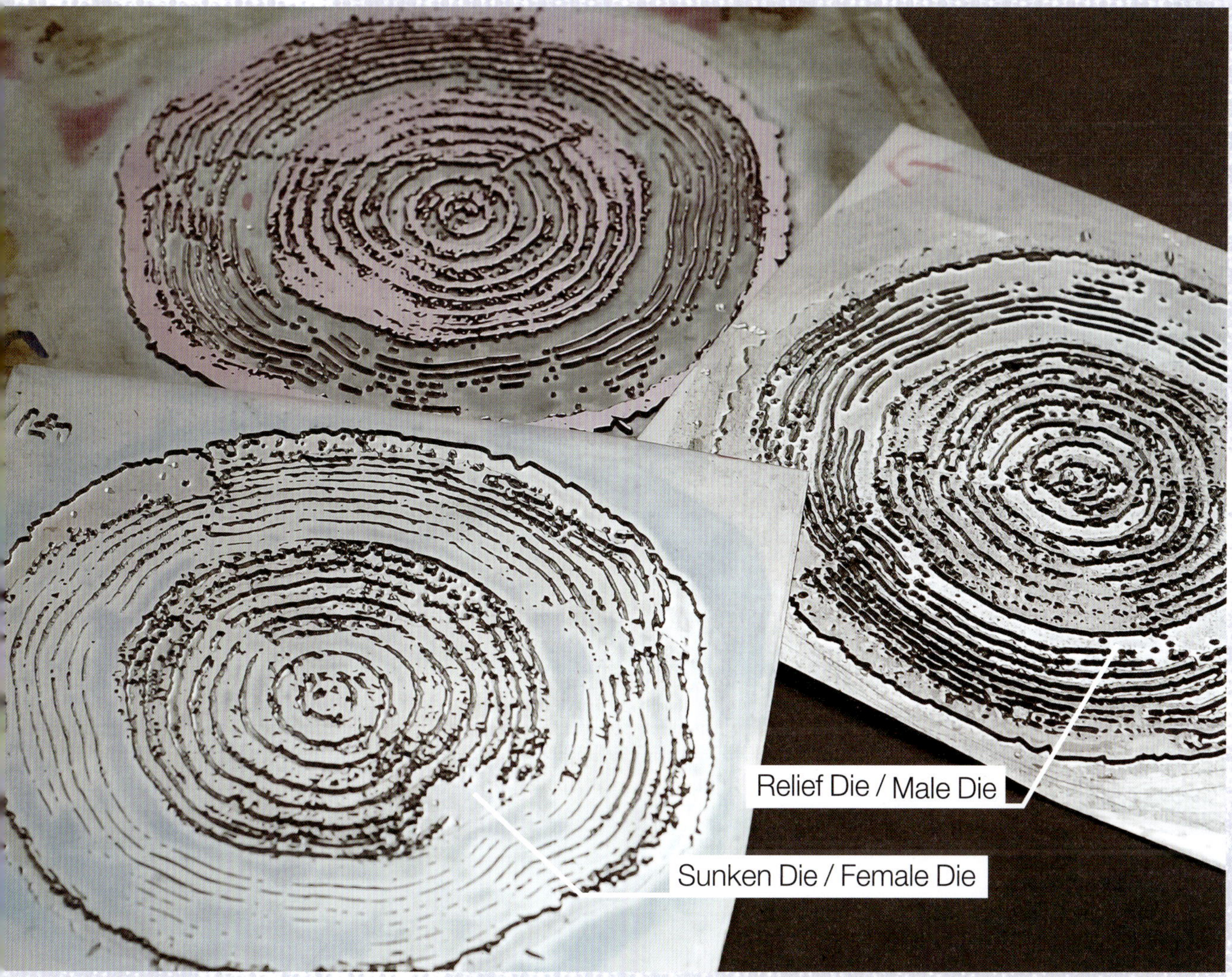

To create various effects and meet different needs, a metal die can be etched in diverse ways. The commonest types are single-level, multi-level, rounded, beveled, and sculptured dies.

Die	Illustration	Features
Single-level	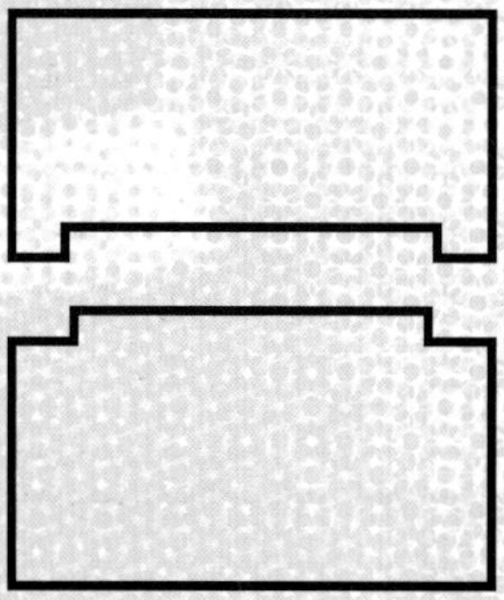	Single-level dies have only one level of depth.
Multi-level	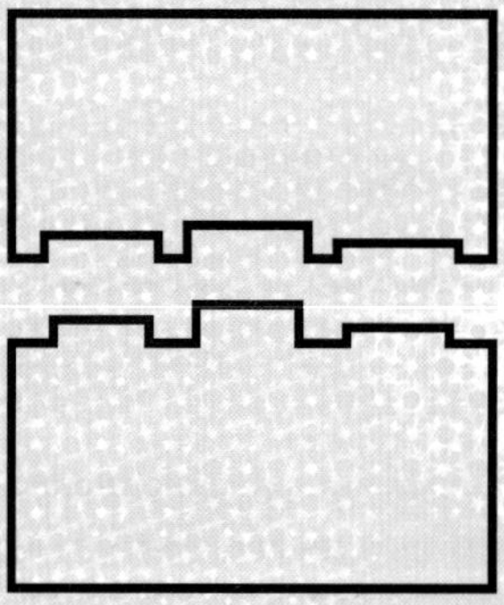	Multi-level dies have more than one level of depth, or perhaps an emboss and deboss together.

Die	Illustration	Features
Rounded (domed)	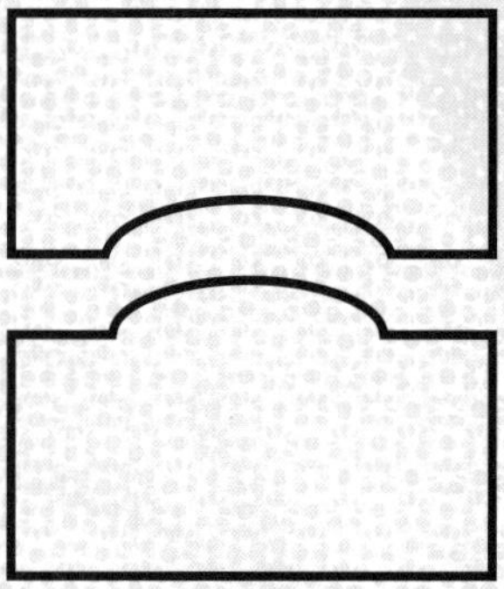	Rounded (domed) dies have rounded edge, often used to create round or elliptical shapes.
Beveled	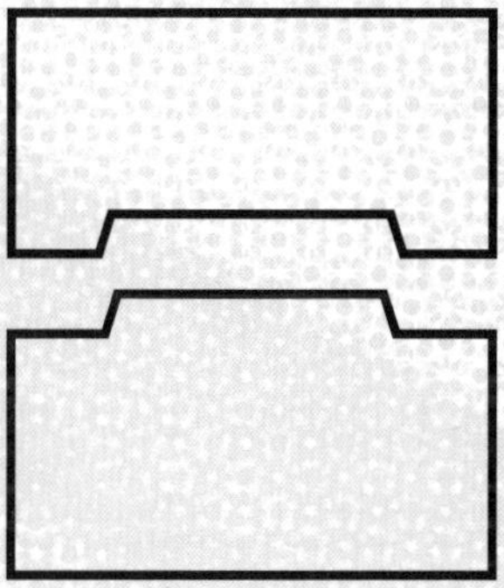	Beveled dies are similar to single-level dies, but display a precise bevel on the image edge. Deeper dies must have beveled edges to prevent cutting through the paper.
Sculptured	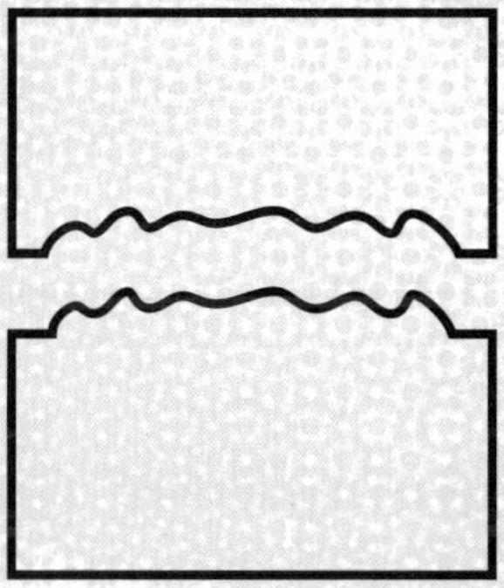	Sculptured dies emboss many levels through the use of curves, angles, and varying depths, contributing detail and dimension to an image.

Stock Selection

Types of Paper is the most common substrate for an emboss or deboss, and the paper's quality will greatly affect the printing result. Thus it is important to choose appropriate paper for your artwork. Thickness, stiffness, and pliability are the three factors you should consider when selecting stock. If paper is too thin and lacks stiffness, the printed image may be blurred. If the paper is insufficiently pliant, it cannot withstand the pressure of embossing and may become torn. So consult with a knowledgeable paper supplier before making a decision.

Tips

1. Generally, embossing requires paper weighted at a minimum of 180g. Thin paper tends to tear when impressed. This, however, is only for your reference, and the decision should depend on what you actually need.

2. Make sure you know the pliability of the paper, because it is a factor that directly affects paper's pressure resistance. So does the thickness of paper, though to a slighter degree.

3. Long-fiber stock is better for embossing and debossing than is short-fiber stock.

4. Recycled stock is not a good choice for embossing and debossing.

Types of Embossing

With the development of technology, more types of embossing have emerged and become popular. Each type has its own characteristics and effects.

Blind Embossing

Blind embossing does not include the use of ink or foil to highlight the embossed area. The raised area results from a pressure on the surface of the paper stock.

Printed Embossing

In this kind of embossing, the embossed area registers with the printed image and is critical to its success.

Textured Embossing

Textured embossing lends a tactile quality to the printed image. Typical textures are pebble or wood grain. Combined with other printing techniques, textured embossing can create an oil-painting effect.

Multi-level Embossing

Laser-cutting dies are used in this kind of embossing. The image area is raised to multiple levels of different depths.

Sculptured Embossing

A sculptured emboss actually refers to a hand tooled process. It is made from a photograph or a drawing with various levels of depth to make the image appear realistic and multi-dimensional.

Combination Embossing

Combination embossing allows for foil stamping and embossing in one press pass. A sculptured die, generally made of brass, is used for this procedure.

2tigers Identity

Design 2tigers

The identity of 2tigers design studio impresses with a strong-contrast color palette: white and bright blue. A brief introduction to the studio, along with a matrix of dots, is raised above the flat stationery, adding a tactile impression.

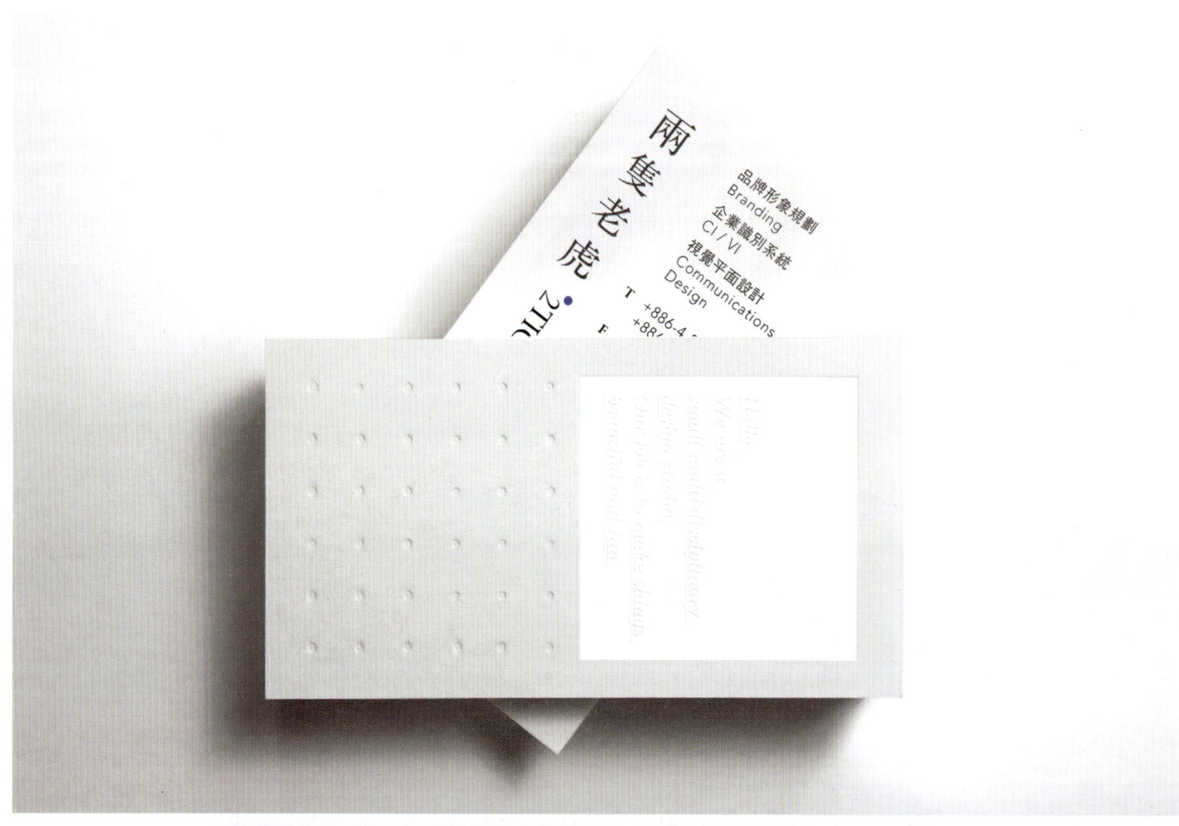

neihang

周洋
创始人 / CEO

+86 181 0189 9948
zhouyang@neihangapp.com
www.neihangapp.com

neihang

Neihang

Design Ori Studio

Neihang is a Shanghai-based, knowledge-sharing community. Fostering links between experts and willing students, the community is home to a diverse range of fields and ideas. The Neihang logo aims to graphically represent the connection between mentor and follower. Therefore, two *N*'s, the initial of the brand, are combined and printed in a raised position, for highlighting. The energetic orange enhances the result.

上海晓行
网络科技有限公司
neihangapp.com

www.neihangapp.com
zhouyang@neihangapp.com
+86 181 0189 9948

DHD Identity

Design MURMURE

Formerly named Billard-Durand, after its founders, DHD Billard-Durand is a French architectural agency in need of a new image. The new logotype, DHD, is formed by the first letter of all three associates' names and, along with the logo mark implying architecture, is used to great effect. Debossing the letters' outline lets the letters and shape stand out. The new identity is also underlined by copper hot stamping, adding depth and elegance to the design.

DHD | Billard-Durand
Architectes

DHD | Billard-Durand
Architectes
DHD | Billard-Durand
Architectes
DHD | Billard-Durand
Architectes
DHD | Billard-Durand
Architectes

FRÉDÉRIC DAVID
Architecte DPLG / Associé
T : 06 30 49 25 69
f.david@dhd-architectes.fr
dhd-architectes.fr
DHD | Billard-Durand
Architectes

SANYI 100 Anniversary

Design Victor Design

SANYI is a honey farm founded in 1915. Upon its 100th anniversary, the company used a customized brochure to make the brand more recognizable. The logo combines the shape of the character 百 (one hundred) and that of a honeycomb. Along with the brand slogan, the logo is debossed in gold on the cover of the brochure, emphasizing the long history and quality of the brand.

SANYI 100
anniversary

三宜、百年蜂華。

Hokusetsu Coffee Roasters

Design Saburo Sakata

This coffee shop is an advocate of coffee culture that values the idea of quietly enjoying a relaxing moment with friends — or alone. Therefore, the packaging resembles the best match for coffee: cookies. Printed in a sunken form, the "cookie" looks more lifelike.

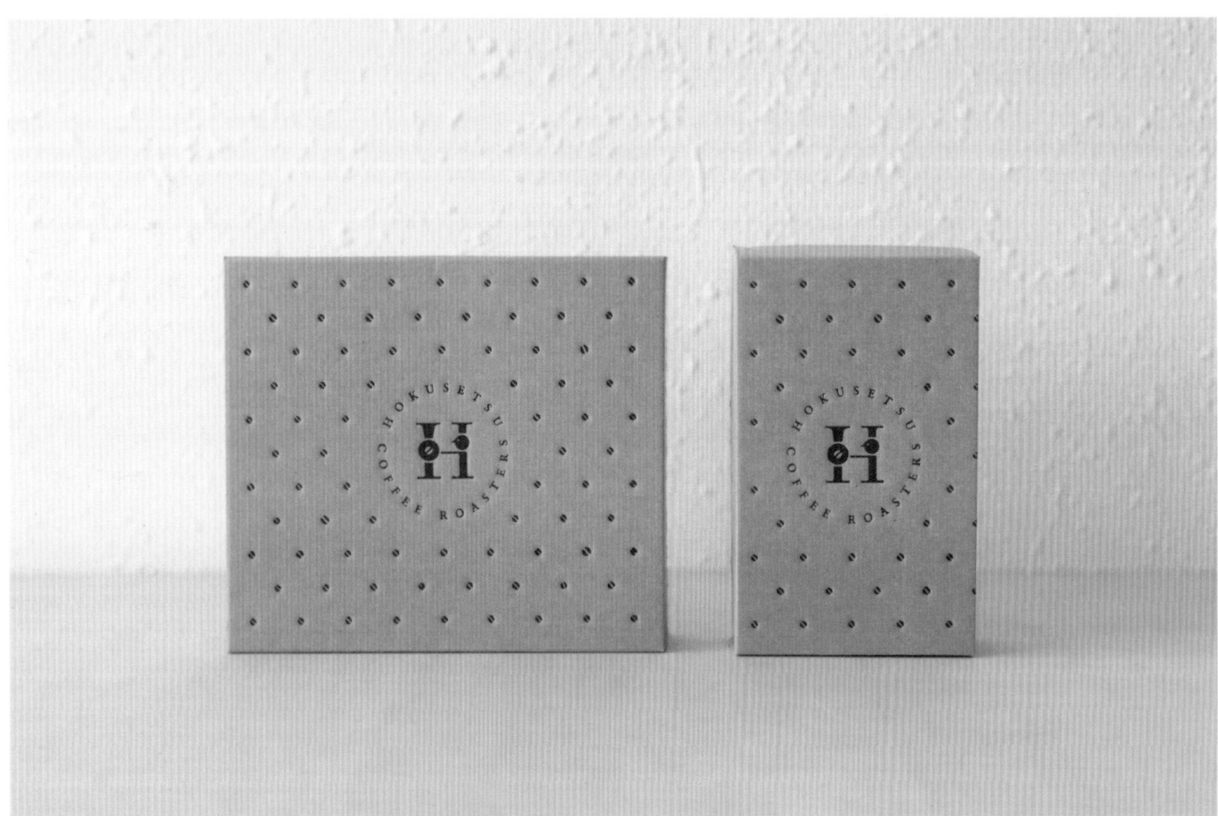

HOKUSETSU COFFEE ROASTERS
北摂焙煎所
Wallman bld. 3F 1-2-20
Senba-Higashi Mino-city
OSAKA JAPAN 562-0035
Tel / Fax 072.726.2266
http://hokusetsu-baisen.com

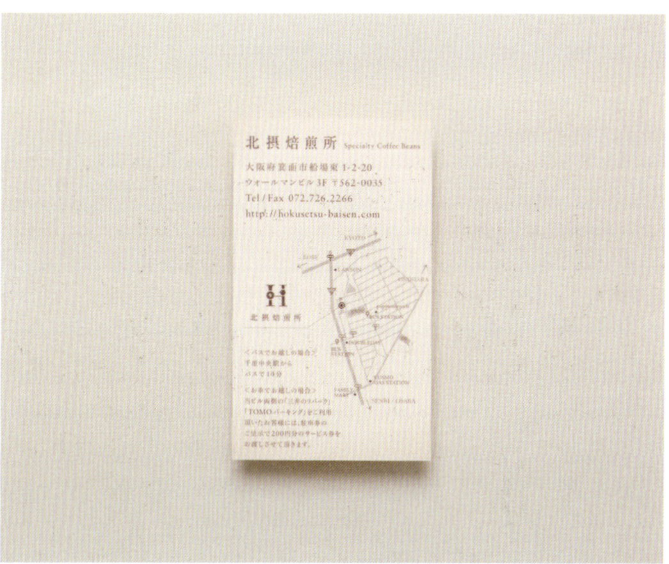
北摂焙煎所 Specialty Coffee Beans
大阪府箕面市船場東 1-2-20
ウォールマンビル 3F 〒562-0035
Tel / Fax 072.726.2266
http://hokusetsu-baisen.com
KYOTO
北摂焙煎所

2016 Letterpress Calendar

Design Fabien Barral

Barral along with a group of graphic designer and typograhers fully used foil stamping and letterpress, bringing a compelling calendar. The calendar, printed by France-based Studio Pression, comes in 2 editions : the special edition comes with a copperplate-printed black cover and foil edging ; the normal edition has a two-color cover printed on white paper, with each page printed in one color, according to the season. The techniques lend a exquisite, artistic look to the work.

THE MORE YOU LOVE YOUR
Decisions
THE LESS YOU NEED
Others
TO LOVE THEM.

Stop thinking about
art works
as objects,
and start thinking about them
as triggers for
experiences.
ONE'S DESTINATION
IS NEVER A PLACE
BUT
A NEW WAY OF SEEING
6
JUNE
7
JULY
EXCUS
THE LITTLE THINGS
ONE DAY
BACK
WERE
LIFE
NOT ABOUT
FINDING

AKE IT
'TIL YOU
AKE IT
THE MORE YOU LOVE YOUR
Decisions
THE LESS YOU NEED
Others
TO LOVE THEM.
2
FEBRUARY
2016
BY BRYAN PATRICK TODD
THERE ARE ONLY
OPTIONS
MAKE
3
MARCH
2016
TRUST
UNEXPECTED
The
EVERYTHING COULD HAPPEN
8
AUGUST

Oishii Kitchen Project

Design Nippon Design Center

This branding is for a revitalization project to introduce new Fukui (a Japanese city) products into the market. As a project named Delicious Kitchen, its branding intends to convey an overall feeling of deliciousness. Appropriately then, such elements as a mouth mark and cookie-shaped paper enhance the stationery design. What further draws the attention is that the invitation and packaging are all printed in relief form to add texture to the patterns. This tactile element contributes to the communicative feel of the stationery design.

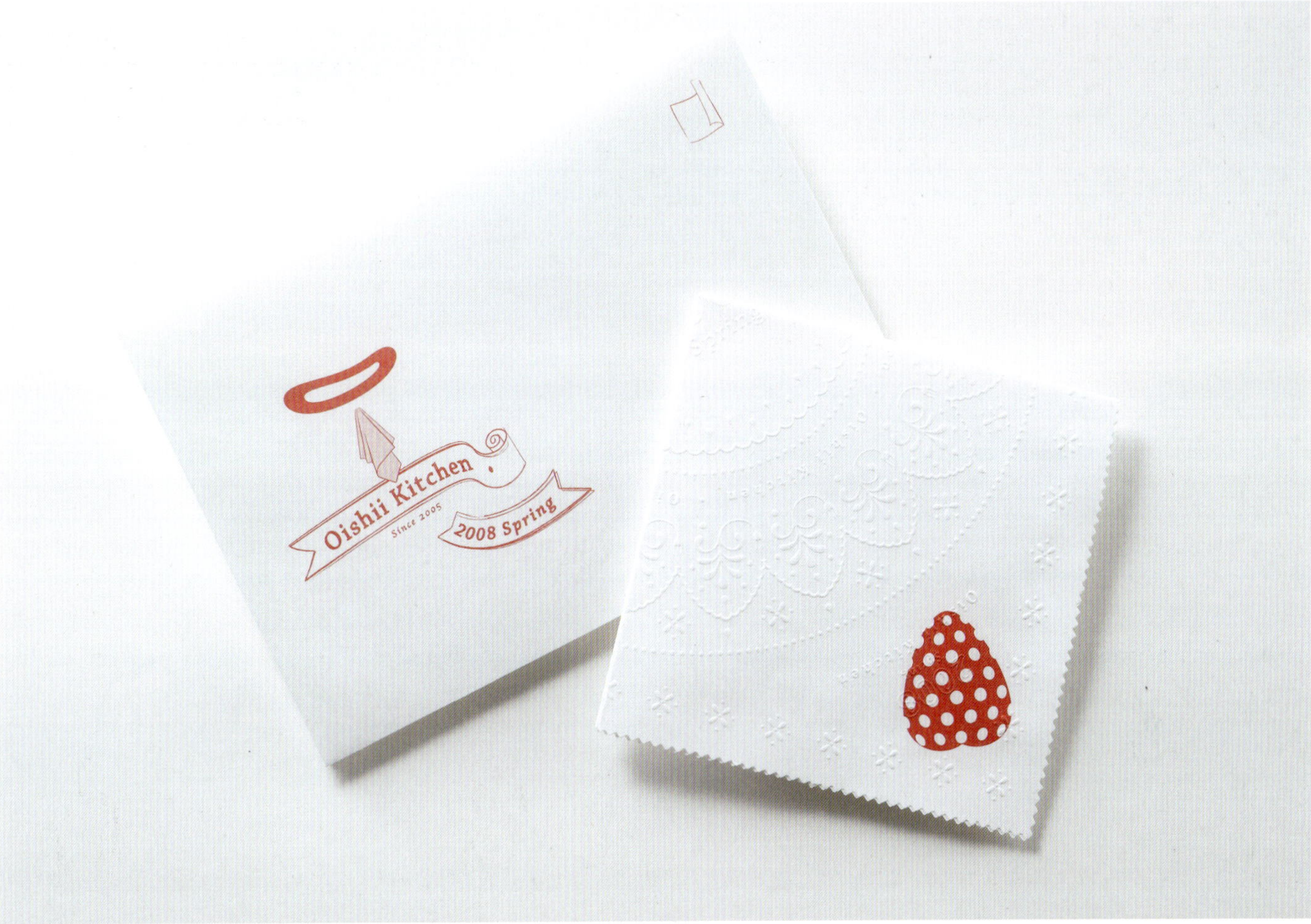
Oishii Kitchen
Since 2005
2008 Spring

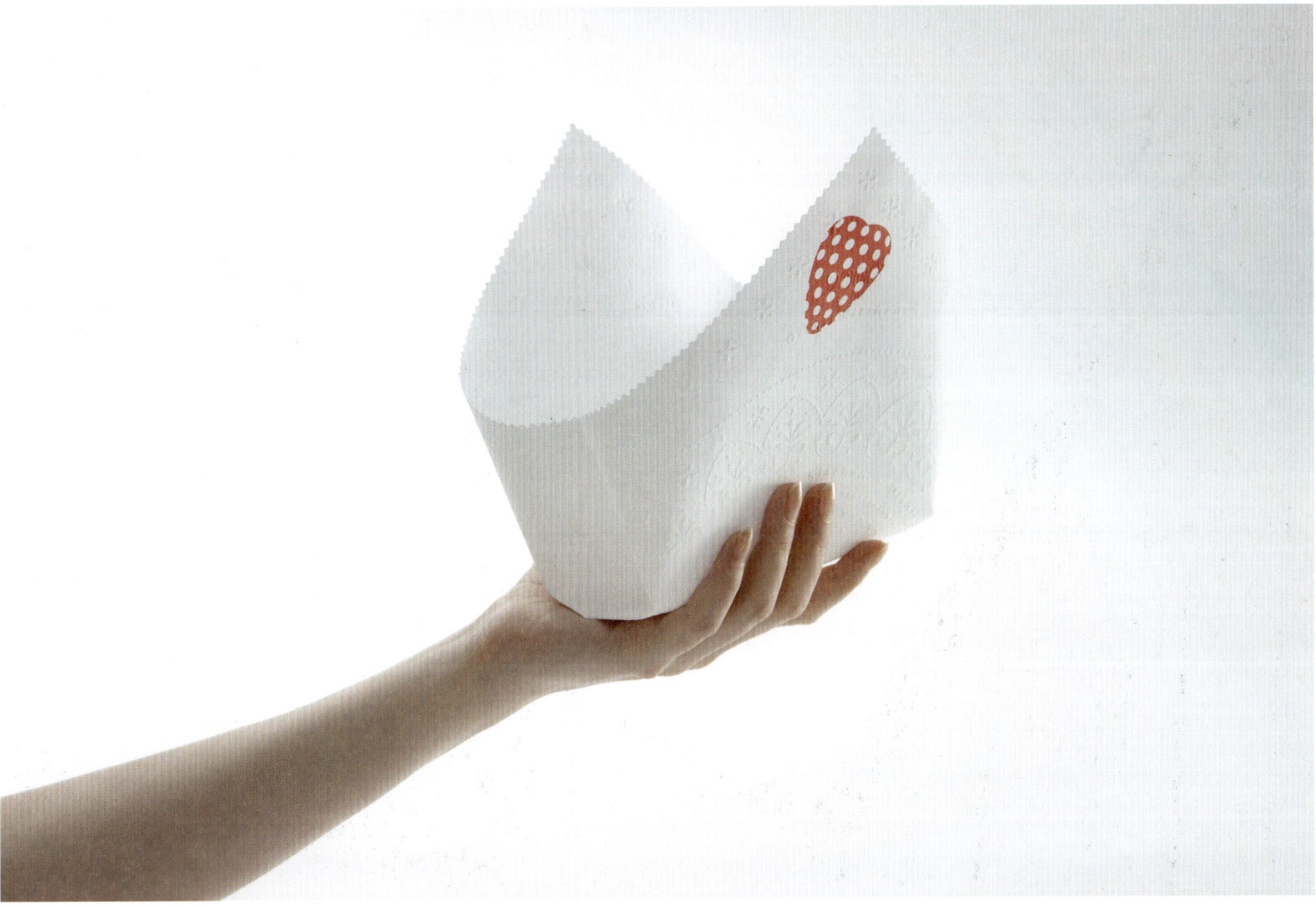

Don Porfirio Branding

Design Kimbal

Don Porfirio is a studio specializing in broadcast design and motion graphic design. The brand required an emblem that could reflect the quality the studio pursues in every project. Kimbal designed a unique monogram by combining the two initials. The minimal design is easily legible even when applied to different platforms and mobile devices at miniscule sizes. When the monogram is used on the business card — regarded as the brand "ambassador" — a printing method generating a strong visual and sensory impact is required. The information appears on cotton paper of 600 grams, with a letterpress finish, which lends the card a robust personality.

DonPorfirio
BROADCAST DESIGN

Taller Estilo Arquitectura Branding

Design Kimbal

This solid and recognizable identity was designed for Taller Estilo Arquitectura, an architectural studio in Merida. The concept was inspired by Le Corbusier's (1887 – 1965) "modulor" and the sketches for the window of Notre Dame du Haut. The symbol was created from a golden ratio rectangle, inside of which an architectonic interior was inscribed to represent the concept of space in its most basic form. The pattern forms an essential part of the identity. Its application on the business card is thus accentuated with a blind embossing, whereas the centered one is lowered, in Cranes Lettra paper of 600 grams. The 3D effect reflects a spatial concept — the nature of the brand — and offers an elegant touch.

TALLER ESTILO
ARQUITECTURA

ARQUI
TECTURA
QUE GENERA
EMOCIONES

VICTOR A. CRUZ DOMÍNGUEZ.
arqvcruz@tallerestiloarquitectura.com
C41 #495 x 58 y 60 Centro.
9273903 / 9997389089.
www.tallerestiloarquitectura.com

TALLER ESTILO
ARQUITECTURA

Casa FS55

Si tuviéramos que describir en una frase el carácter de la casa FS55 podríamos resumir que "es una vivienda con espíritu moderno".

Aunque la vivienda original data de los años que el modernismo estaba en su apogeo, la estructura original mucho distaba de poseer característica alguna de la arquitectura de la época, por el contrario existía un dominio de muros sólidos y pesados, pocas aperturas con poca o nula integración al exterior.

La intervención retoma la premisa del modernismo renovando el carácter de la vivienda integrando conceptos de mayor funcionalidad al igual de nuevos materiales que complementan los tradicionales preexistentes.

El resultado es una vivienda renovada, llena de luz e inundada de ventilación natural, que retoma la estética del movimiento moderno con líneas puras y simples sin dejar atrás la estética de la arquitectura regional, integrando materiales tradicionales vistos desde una nueva estética, pisos brillantes y coloridos de cemento contrastan con muros neutros que son el lienzo perfecto para el arte y el mobiliario.

Al exterior los muros existentes exhiben su materia prima contrastando la naturalidad de la piedra con el carácter industrial del concreto.

El anexo posterior surge tan simple como agregar una cubierta que se asienta en los muros laterales y define un espacio que se complementa definiendo sus límites con muros de cristal, que resguardan el espacio interior y permiten la integración del espacio exterior.

Atentamente:

Victor A. Cruz
Víctor A. Cruz.
Arquitecto.

927903/ 99997389089
contacto@tallerestiloarquitectura.com

Calle 41#495 x 58y 60 Centro,Mérida,Yucatán.
tallerestiloarquitectura.com

TALLER ESTILO
ARQUITECTURA

Clara & Daniel Wedding Invitation

Design El Calotipo Printing Studio

Clara and Daniel are musicians. The instruments they play are made up of stressed geometric shapes and beautiful curves. These elements are blended into their wedding invitation to add a personal touch: a chocolate "cover" decorated by an elaborate raised-rosette pattern.

Clara Paúl &
Daniel Zapico
CD

Clara Paúl &
Daniel Zapico
14 de septiembre de 2013 | El Llantén (Valladolid)

Anni Hall

Design Daniel Dittmar

Anni Hall is an Australian creative working across a diverse range of disciplines including beauty, makeup, and writing. Her branding uses flowers coming from various environments that have influenced her practice. Their scents overflow the printed stationery to suggest — through sight and scent — the places related to Anni. The information, embossed on the stock with subtle colors, appears both simple and classic.

Anand's Business Card

Design Anand Design

Anand is a member of Generation Press (GP). His very first card was printed on GP Colorplan Brarry, with 350gsm stock and a gravure-printed personal logo to enhance the tactile experience.

500920
24/03/2010
ANAND
24/03/2010
500920

24/03/2010
We are carbon neutral
Using FSC paper
Anand
Graphic Design & Illustration
Tel +44 (0)7762 533 206
Email hello@anand-design.com
Web www.anand-design.com

The Artling

Design Foreign Policy Design Group

The Artling is an online gallery showcasing limited-edition prints from a curated group of artists, photographers, image-makers, and designers. The identity takes its inspiration from a warehouse sheltering art pieces; the gold borders are reminiscent of gilded frames. The use of the curator/ founder's handwriting in blue ink in the stationery gives the identity an added personal touch. Each art piece is carefully and meticulously selected. The initial of Artling is highlighted in an embossed form atop a red seal.

Badaboom

Design Kind

Badaboom is an emerging company producing soft textiles made from bamboo. Thus, the identity uses the symbol of bamboo as its main element. Intaglio printed, the minimalist logo is further underlined on the stock. Playfully, the identity adopts a rich and soft color palette.

badaboom

Coffee Card

Design Lumír Kajnar

Jakub Hartl is dedicated to the world of coffee. His business card features simply a graphic coffee cup on a brown background. The cup is varnished to provide a glazed-pottery effect. From the area directly above the cup rises the owner's embossed name and contact number, like a fragrant vapor from the brew: a simple and unique design.

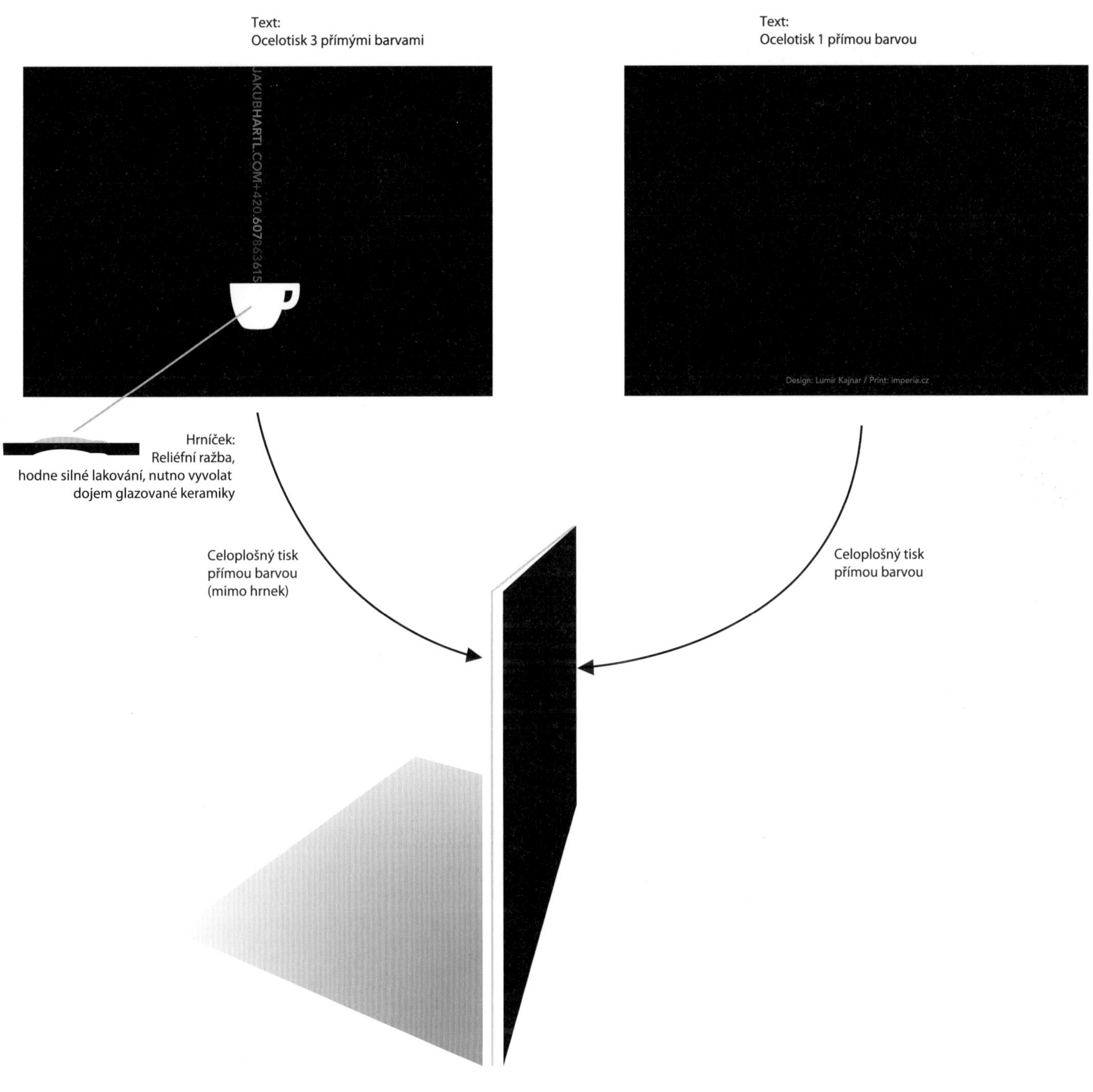
Text:
Ocelotisk 3 přímými barvami
Text:
Ocelotisk 1 přímou barvou
JAKUBHARTL.COM+420.607863615
Design: Lumír Kajnar / Print: imperia.cz
Hrníček:
Reliéfní ražba,
hodne silné lakování, nutno vyvolat
dojem glazované keramiky
Celoplošný tisk
přímou barvou
(mimo hrnek)
Celoplošný tisk
přímou barvou
2 slepené bílé papíry
hmotnost: 250–350 g/m²

Wolfensson Fashion Identity

Design VON K Design

The exclusive fashion store Wolfensson moved its high-quality designer pieces to a former print shop, as a new salesroom. Thus a completely new visual image was created that emphasized black and white. The debossing logotype on the stationery helps attract attention.

W_

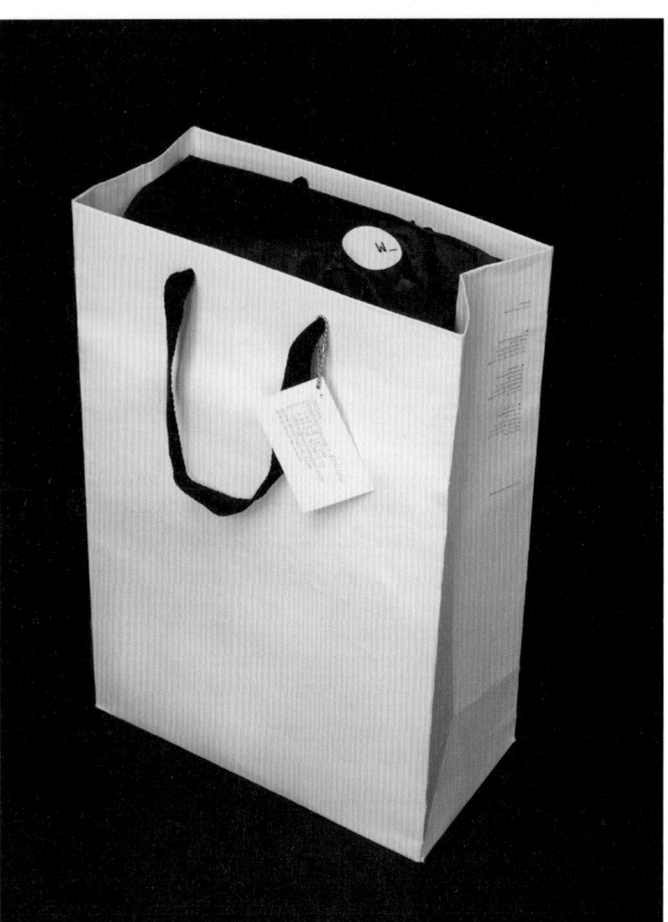

Identity for Dronninga Landskap

Design Dinamo Design

To offer a clear position in a competitive market, Dronninga Landskap, a Norwegian landscape architecture firm, needed a new identity. The symbol of a garden maze was chosen as a key element in the identity to emphasize tradition and craftsmanship. The image further represents Dronninga Landskap's way of thinking: as a symbol of how they approach their projects. The embossed pattern mimics the tactility of a garden maze in nature, also important in their identity.

ANE H. ØVERLIE
landskapsarkitekt
t +47 40 62 64 22
m +47 93 44 79 92 [privat]
e aov@dronninga-landskap.no
w dronninga-landskap.com
Dronninga landskap as
Prinsens gate 6
N-0152 Oslo

Grafiko Rebranding

Design Toormix

Grafiko, a printing company, updated its identity on the occasion of its tenth anniversary. The rebranding plays with a *K*, the letter that stands out in the name Grafiko. The shape looks like a wood type used in old printers, suggesting Grafiko's services. The graphic applications always feature a *K* pattern in various printed forms.

Yellow
autograph
hunter
famous
celebrity
signature
postcard
signature postcards collection
sponsored by
grafiko

Diffraction Business Cards

Design DMWORKROOM

Julien Hauchecorne is a Paris-based art dealer specializing in retro furniture and decorative art from 1970s. His business cards have been letterpress printed with deep debossing of the logo on thick 700gsm card stock. The edge with diffraction effect enhances an eye-catching look.

Julien Hauchecorne
102 rue de Sèvres
75015 Paris
+33 (0)9 51 72 27 72
+33 (0)6 74 56 52 82
info@julienhauchecorne.com
www.julienhauchecorne.com

Book Design for Control

Design SNASK

The book's title, *Control-Effect Communication and the Battle for Our Thoughts*, written by Erik Modig, suggests that the subject is communication. The book design looks timeless, yet modern classic, and its cover contributes to this appeal. In fact, only two colors are used, and their contrast makes for a clean and outstanding presentation. The embossed brain shape echoes the book's title and offers a tactile cover.

STIMULANS
ENGAGEMANG
RELEVANS
KANSLOR
NYSKAPANDE
IDENTIFIERING
EMOTIONELL REAKTION
UPPREPNING
HEURISTICS
KONCEPTUALISERING
ASIKTER 3.
ASSOCIATIONER 2.
SYNLIGHET 1.
EMOTIONELL REAKTION 2.
RUTIN HEURISTICS 1.
1. RUTIN
2. KANSLOR
3. TANKAR

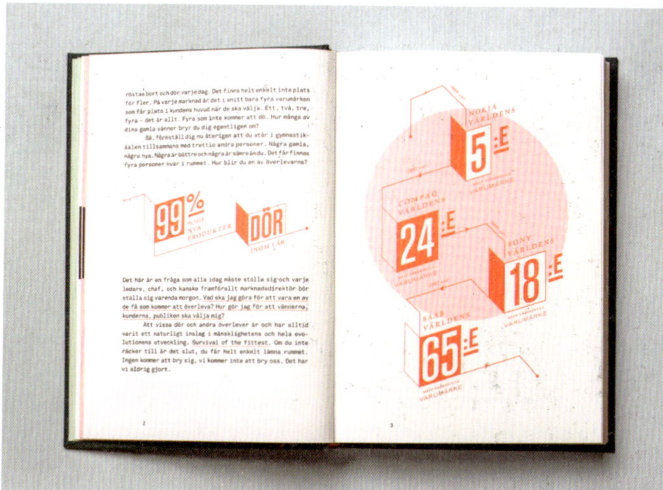
99%
DÖR
5:E
24:E
18:E
65:E

Letterpress Business Cards

Design Fabien Barral

Fabien Barral is a graphic designer who enjoys designing various cards printed in letterpress.

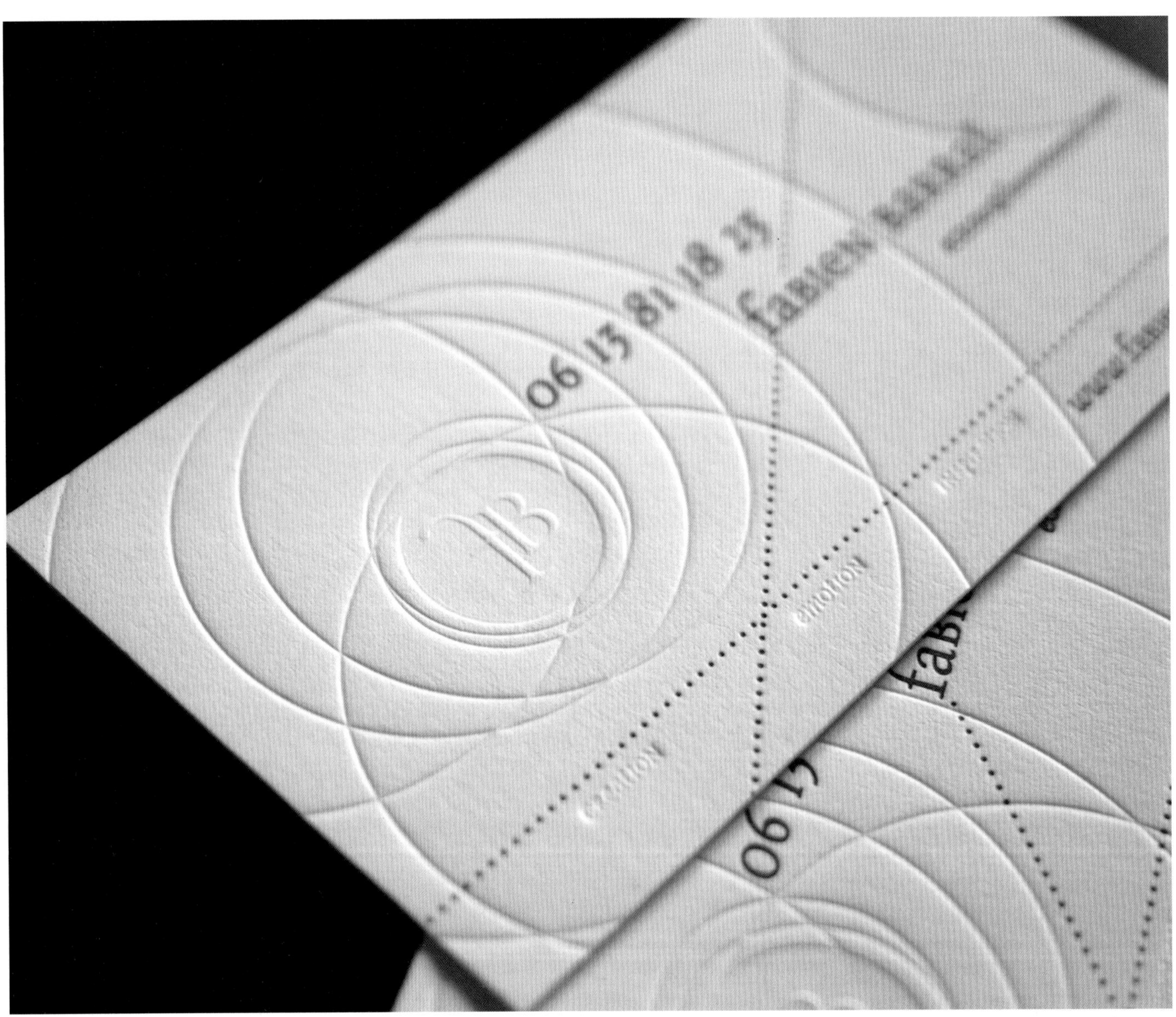

The 2009 edition: Inspired by the ripple effect we see when we touch water, Fabien mimics the pattern on the card to communicate the message that whatever we do ripples beyond the initial action.

The 2010 edition: Fabien wants the card to reflect his own identity by incorporating splash and shapes painted by his wife Frédérique, who is an inspiration in Fabien's life and work.

The 2011 edition: These are experimental cards. When you put two colors on the same roller of a press, one on each end, it allows them to blend naturally in the middle, creating a gradient across the press sheet. Fabien tested several color combinations for this series.

Mathias Tanguy Brand Identity

Design DMWORKROOM

As a personal finance adviser, Mathias Tanguy needed an identity emphasizing networking, communication, and professional ethics and principles.

DMWORKROOM designed a visual identity around a geometrical pattern that is now creating network connectivity for Mathias. Placing the letters in the center of each of the graphic polygonal shapes allowed the name to form the core of the geometrical network pattern. Extracting the letters *M* and *T* with their surrounding polygonal structures created a logotype working as an ingenuous monogram. This simple shape allows the use of many different high-finish print processes, such as the new leather-and-metal embossed surfaces on the business card sides and the stamped seal on the envelope.

M A
T A

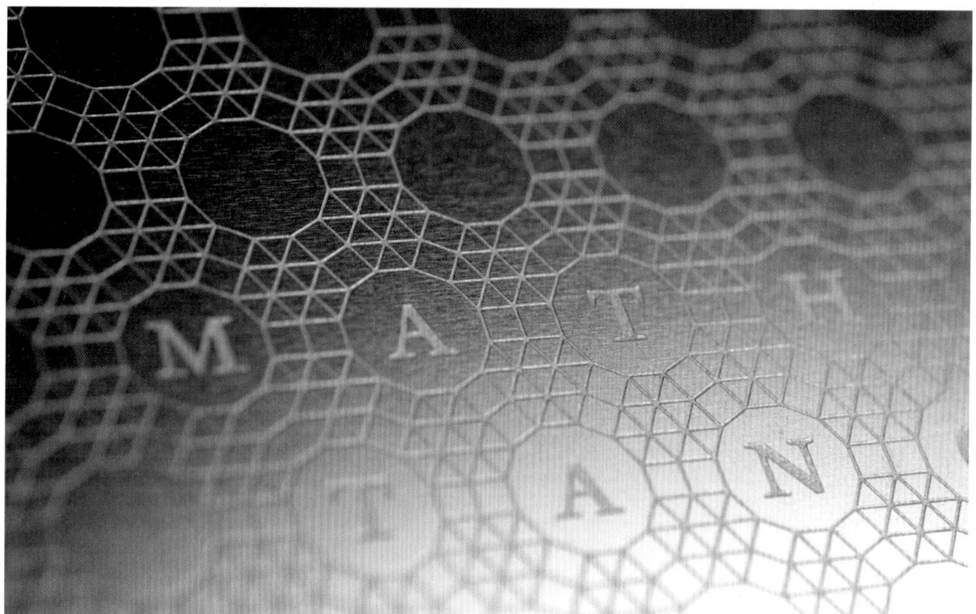
M A T
T A N

H I A S

M A T H I A S
T A N G U Y
M. T.
S

M A T H
T A N
Mathias Tanguy
Fiscaliste
Cabinet Exell Finance
Ingénierie fiscale
06 68 40 03 11
mtanguy@exellfinance.com

Neenah Character

Design Design Army

This set showcases a multitude of Neenah Packaging papers with flowing dyelines and eye-catching printing techniques. Neenah explores the possibilities of paper while showing designers that a compelling design requires quality paper and appropriate printing technology.

The benefits of paper recycling are in line with the values behind sustainable housing. They include: extending the supply of wood fiber; reducing greenhouse gas emission; contributing to carbon sequestration; and saving considerable landfill space.
W
OR
LD

Oblique Business Card

Design Philippe Cossette

Oblique, a visual-effects company from Montreal, needed to update their logo and stationery. Philippe Cossette thought of a concept where the logo would reveal itself when viewed from a different perspective: a shape that would otherwise look trivial. This is the way Oblique deals with each new project.

The design of the business card reflects this concept. It folds itself into the company's logo. The raised-printed logo on the card works well with this concept of two-dimension to three-dimension.

OBLIQUE
ASHLEE LYNN WISMACH
VFX Producer
awismach@obliquefx.com
t. 514.844.2500 ext.133
c. 514.928.7188
f. 514.844.2509
1470 Peel, Tower B
Suite 910, Montréal
Québec Canada
H3A 1T1 Obliquefx.com

NINE Identity Design

Design Roots

NINE is a new photography studio. When designing the website and identity, Roots highlighted the studio space as the core element. The identity is conceptually derived from the floor space, which then is developed into an iterative golden-ratio rectangle logo mark. This logo mark resembles a floorplan drawing, with the iterations within the rectangle corresponding loosely to the actual floor space divisions. The debossed edges of the rectangles add to the sense of space.

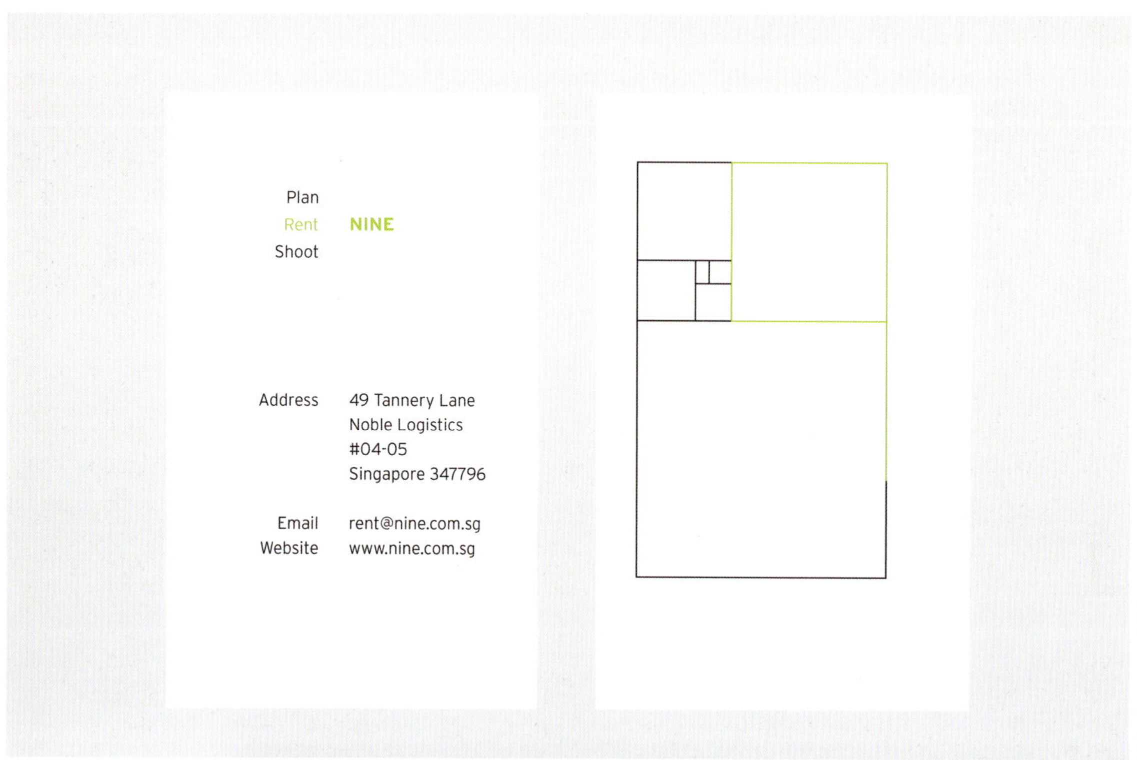

ReARTlity Show

Design HOUTH

ReARTlity Show is a non-traditional exhibition which shows the audience the process of making arts instead of displaying finished artworks, which is like a live performance. Its brochure was designed to reveal this concept, being folded into a triangle shape. Some elements of its illustration were embossed to add tactility.

Book Design: Recollection

Design ACST Design

Recollection is a special issue featuring the achievements of the Taiwan e-Learning and Digital Archives Program, conducted by the Institute of History and Philology of Academia Sinica, Taiwan. The set consists of a publication along with a jacket poster and a manga booklet. The embossed annual-ring imagery on both front and back covers symbolizes the program's achievements of the past ten years while modulating the title's message to suggest that every project and all research in the book are memorable parts of the whole process.

Tjuvholmen Sjømagasin

Design Work in Progress

Tjuvholmen Sjømagasin is a seafood restaurant located in a waterfront area of central Oslo, Norway. For the amusement of elderly seamen, the front of the business card displays the cardholder's name in Morse code. Front right appears a multi-level embossing of sea shells and imaginary creatures mentioned in some myths of the sea. The logo (back) is made with oceanic, wavy typography.

Eine Branding

Design Root

Ben Eine is a famous street artist who specializes in the central element of all graffiti — the forms of letters. He needed a brand that could translate across all platforms—appealing to his collectors and the world's greatest galleries.

Design agency Root combined the black paint drips that Eine uses on the edges of his unique canvases with one of Eine's signature typefaces, the Circus font, in the form of an embossed *E*. The simple and elegant result highlights Eine's stunning work.

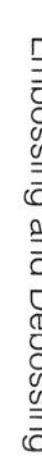

Sophia Georgopoulou Identity

Design Sophia Georgopoulou

Sophia Georgopoulou's name card is printed using the debossing method, on thick, recycled paper. All the information is printed without colors. She also designs round stickers carrying different messages and uses them on the name card for personality. As a result, each business card is unique.

sophiag
.com
sophiag
.com

Food.Chocolate.Design

Design Happycentro

Happycentro designed this publication to reflect the inspirations, recipes, and texts from the 2013 Pitti's Taste fair in Florence. For the book cover, featuring a food theme, the designers used paper with a natural feeling. Embossing for, the book title is highlighted.

FOOD.
CHOCOLATE.
DESIGN.
1 CHOCOLATE MAKER
8 FOOD CRAFTSMEN
8 FOOD BLOGGERS
16 SPECIAL RECIPES
16 GRAPHIC DESIGNERS
1 COLLECTIVE PROJECT

Pfeffersack & Soehne Spice Packaging

Design Pfeffersack & Soehne

The aesthetically packed spices by Pfeffersack & Soehne achieve perfect flavor preservation. The discreet design has a timeless appeal and looks stunning. The tops of each packaging box and can are embossed with the Pfeffersack & Soehne logotype and its monogram, applied in solid black color, which offers simple elegance.

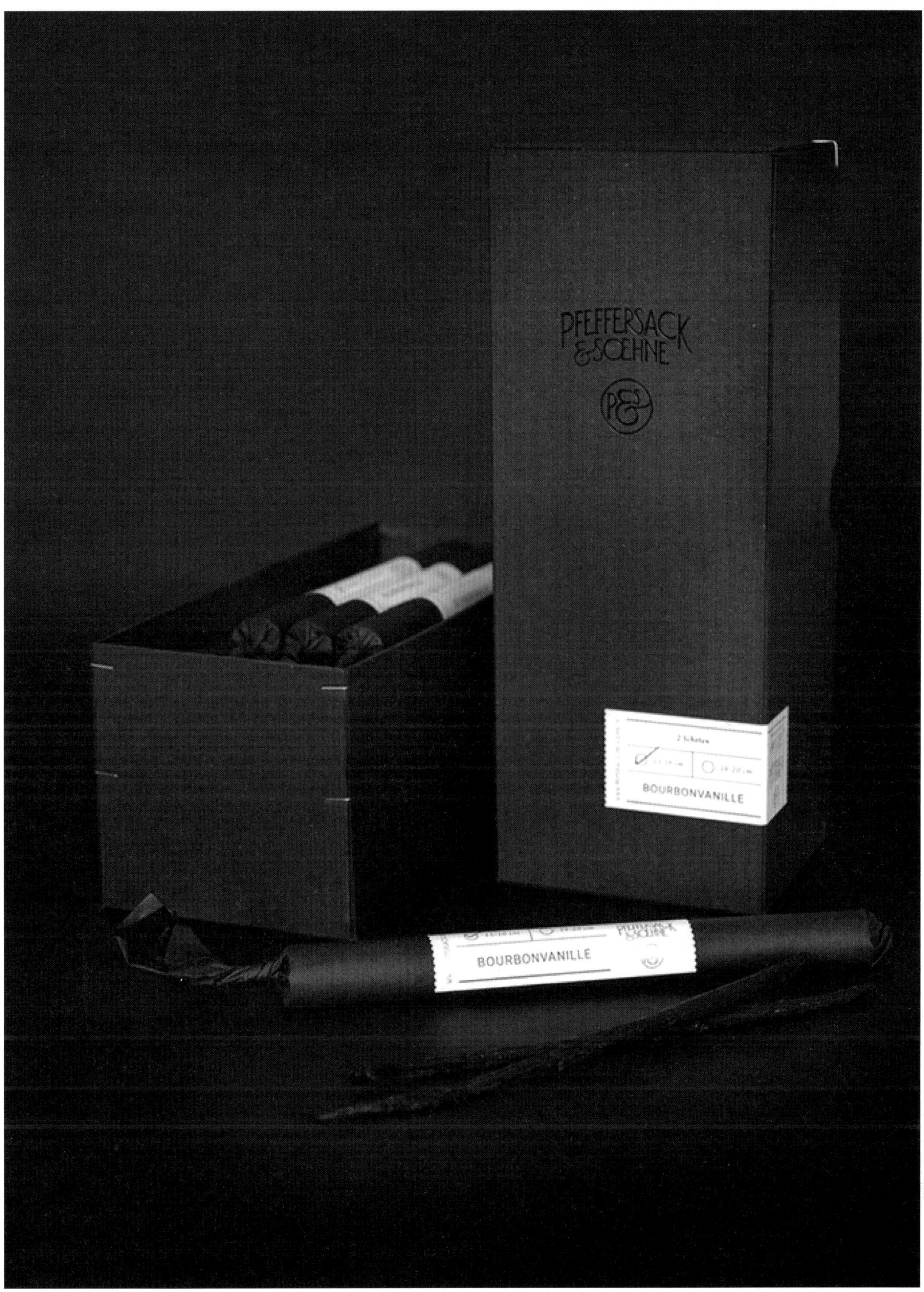
PFEFFERSACK
&SOEHNE
BOURBONVANILLE
BOURBONVANILLE

BVD Rebranding

Design BVD

BVD is a design-and-branding agency specializing in strategic design. The design team created a new identity for themselves, reflecting their ambitions and representing their quality standard. The logo is easily recognizable, with clean, geometrical lines and is applied to the name cards in a raised form, against other, debossed, information. The printing techniques lend the cards a bit of depth.

Carin Blidholm Svensson
Creative Director
Founder
Åsögatan 115
carin@bvd.se
bvd.se
BVD

Bookmark the
new bvd.se

BVD
Carin Blidholm Svensson
Creative Director
Founder
Åsögatan 115
116 24 Stockholm Sweden
+46 (0)8 660 00 57
+46 (0)70 535 50 55
carin@bvd.se
bvd.se
Catrin Vägnemark
Creative Director
Founder
Åsögatan 115
116 24 Stockholm Sweden
+46 (0)8 660 00 57
+46 (0)70 862 14 70
catrin@bvd.se
bvd.se

Longmark

Design Shenzhen Huathink Design Company

Longmark is a group founded by a batch of outstanding Chinese scientists and marketing specialists. Working with United Gene, it is dedicated to the promotion of gene technology, products, and services. To emphasize this theme, Huathink Design uses blue linen cloth on the cover of the group's brochure, resembling genetic combination. The texture spices up the design with more tactility.

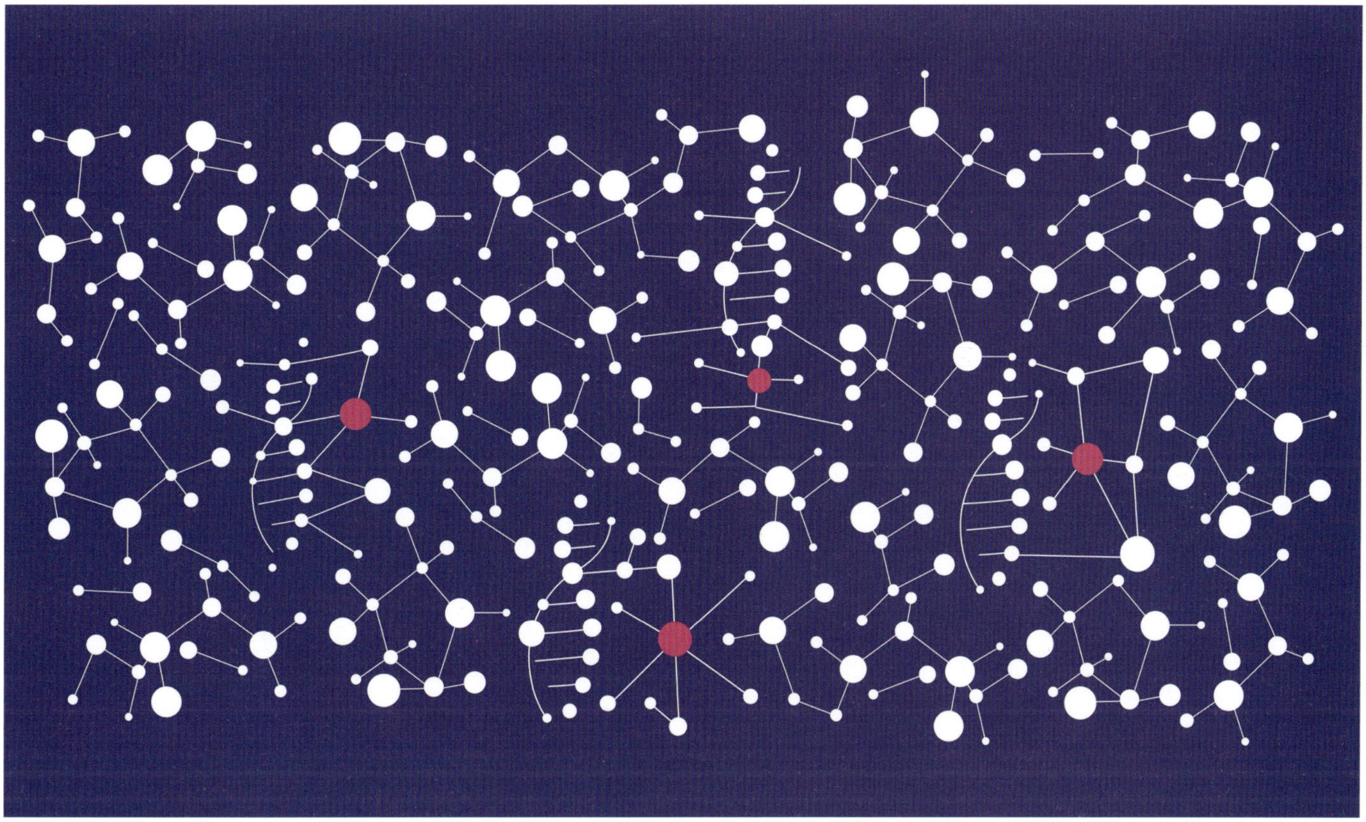

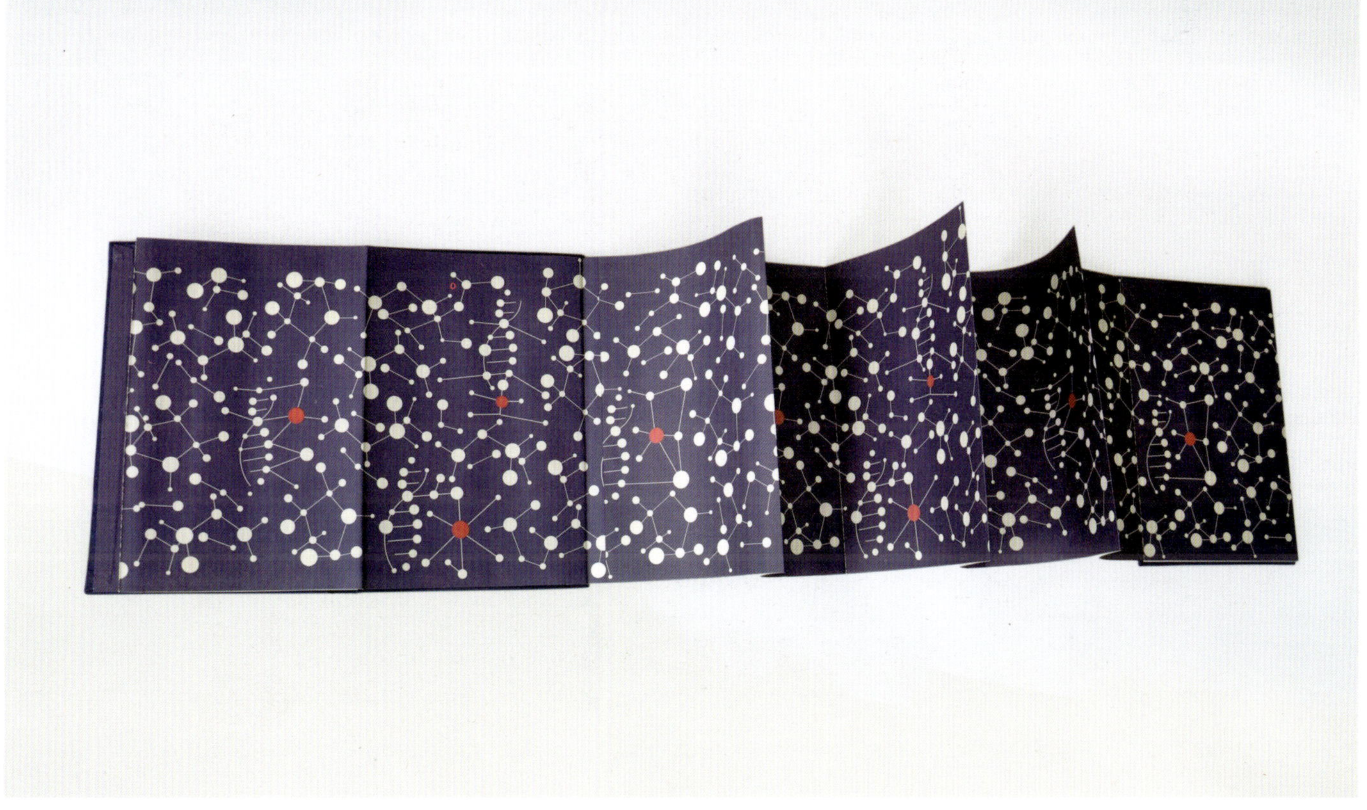

INDEX

ACKNOWLEDGEMENTS

We would like to thank all the designers and contributors who have been involved in the production of this book; their contributions have been indispensable to its creation. We would also like to express our gratitude to all the producers for their invaluable opinions and assistance throughout this project. And to the many others whose names are not credited but have made helpful suggestions, we thank you for your continuous support.

FUTURE PARTNERSHIPS

If you wish to participate in SendPoints' future projects and publications, please send your website or portfolio to editor01@sendpoints.cn.